color

The African American Intellectual Heritage

Paul Spickard and Patrick Miller,
Series Editors

Kenneth A. McClane

color

Essays on Race, Family, and History

University of Notre Dame Press · Notre Dame, Indiana

Published by the University of Notre Dame Press
Notre Dame, Indiana 46556
www.undpress.nd.edu

Library of Congress Cataloging-in-Publication Data
McClane, Kenneth A., 1951–
Color : essays on race, family, and history / Kenneth A.
McClane.
    p.   cm. — (The African American intellectual heritage)
ISBN-13: 978-0-268-03515-0 (pbk. : alk. paper)
ISBN-10: 0-268-03515-6 (pbk. : alk. paper)
1. McClane, Kenneth A., 1951–   2. African American poets—
Biography.   3. African Americans—Social conditions—1975–
I. Title.
PS3563.A26119Z46   2009
814'.54—dc19
                                2008051320

For Rochelle

Books by Kenneth A. McClane

poetry

Running Before the Wind

Out Beyond the Bay

Moons and Low Times

To Hear the River

At Winter's End

These Halves Are Whole

A Tree Beyond Telling: Selected Poems

Take Five: Collected Poems, 1971–1986

essays

Walls: Essays, 1985–1990

Color: Essays on Race, Family, and History

Contents

The McClane Family

(from left: Adrienne, Paul, Genevieve, Kenneth, and Kenneth, Jr.)

Acknowledgments

I would like to thank the editors of the following publications in which these essays first appeared: *Bookpress,* for "A Love Note: A. R. Ammons as Teacher"; *English Department Newsletter,* for "Hungers: Reflections on Affirmative Action"; and *Epoch,* for "The Mitchell Movement," "The 13th Juror," and "Color."

"Shadow Boxing," © The Antioch Review, Inc., first appeared in the *Antioch Review,* vol. 58, no. 4, Fall 2000. Reprinted by permission of the editors.

"Teachers," © The Antioch Review, Inc., first appeared in the *Antioch Review,* vol. 60, no. 1, Winter 2002. Reprinted by permission of the editors.

"A King's Holiday: A Personal Reminiscence of Dr. Martin Luther King, Jr.," © The Antioch Review, Inc., first appeared in the *Antioch Review,* vol. 60, no. 4, Fall 2002. Reprinted by permission of the editors.

"Musicals," © The Antioch Review, Inc., first appeared in the *Antioch Review,* vol. 63, no. 4, Fall 2005. Reprinted by permission of the editors.

"Driving," © The Antioch Review, Inc., first appeared in the *Antioch Review,* vol. 64, no. 4, Fall 2006. Reprinted by permission of the editors.

acknowledgments

I would also like to thank David Burak and Rodger Gilbert for reprinting "A Love Note: A. R. Ammons as Teacher" in their fine book, *Considering the Radiance: Essays on the Poetry of A. R. Ammons* (W. W. Norton & Company, 2005).

A slightly revised version of "The Mitchell Movement" was published in *After the Bell: Contemporary American Prose about School,* edited by Maggie Anderson and David Hessler (University of Iowa Press, 2007).

I would also like to thank the *Antioch Review* for honoring me with the 2002 Distinguished Prose Award.

And I would be remiss if I did not thank Barbara Hanrahan, the superb director of the University of Notre Dame Press, who called me three days after she had read two of the essays included here. A writer needs to be corroborated, and that call, at a rather dark time for me, was life itself.

Introduction

I began writing essays when my brother, Paul, died of alcoholism in 1982. By then, I had published six books of poems and had found poetry to be a safe harbor for my enthusiasms. Before 1982, I didn't like sentences; they tended to go awry, and I wasn't, in all honesty, self-confident enough in my own announcements to assail prose. Yet Paul's death changed everything. In fact, I have only composed one poem since his loss—and it, interestingly, had to do with September 11, 2001, which, of course, was another great tragedy, with enormous resonance for me, a displaced New Yorker.

After Paul's death, something inexorably perished in me. It was the sense that the world could continue in the same vein, that what I had done before could survive. Heretofore, poetry for me was a sacred calling: the highest of the Arts. My difficult love for my brother—and it was blustery, indeed—involved the same spiritual anchoring. With his death went my desire to compose poetry. And yet I am a writer. And as a writer, I can only understand the world, alas, by writing about it.

Walls, my first collection of essays, appeared in 1991. It took seventeen years to complete this second book. During the interim, both of my parents died of Alzheimer's disease, the world grew meaner, and I kept trying to write the best I could. Some people climb mountains, others reimagine the laws of physics; a writer, simply, writes. And for a black writer, authorship takes on even more salience. Historically, black people in much of the United States were not permitted to learn to read or write. Indeed, writing was a crime, and slaves were often murdered for attempting to master the alphabet. But we, as Frederick Douglass beautifully affirms, wrote ourselves into personhood, and often with a grace unmatched in American letters. And so, in every class I teach at Cornell, I tell my students—white and black alike—to write, write, write. It is not a matter of choice: it is a matter of *existence*.

There are essays here about Dr. Martin Luther King, Jr.'s visit to our cottage in Martha's Vineyard, my mother's odyssey to have her racial designation changed on her birth certificate, and my father's difficult struggle as a black student to gain admittance to medical school in the 1930s, even though he graduated second in his class, in three years, from Boston University, with a major in chemistry. There is a reminiscence about teaching the profoundly handicapped at a superb public school; an essay about my parents' mutual drift into Alzheimer's disease; a paean to my parents' love for musicals; a disquisition on affirmative action; and a love note to the great poet A. R. Ammons, who taught me much.

All of these essays concern race, although they, like the human spirit, wildly sweep and yaw. Since many of these essays were written as discrete pieces, they demand, as any self-reliant organism must, much contextual foregrounding; and so you will read about my father's life, from numerous vantage points, in various essays. If they work, these essays attempt to celebrate how experience triangulates: how life, like a diamond, is the sum of its facets, each experience presenting a discrete shimmering, each, in some particularized way, amending and refracting the overall luminosity. For this reason, I often withhold bits of the narrative, for example, when

I discuss my father's medical school experience. In one essay you learn a great deal about his travail; in another, there's an added insight, a slight qualification, a detail previously withheld. Some of this is intentional, having to do with narrative force and drama; some of this, truthfully, has to do with my own penchant for self-involvement. And some of this, of course, celebrates how the memory works. I hope these moments of narrative recapitulation are not too distracting.

Memory, of course, refines and recalibrates, and this is a book about recollection, which is to say, it is a book about inference. To have two parents die of Alzheimer's is to understand—and powerfully—the constitutive value of memory. We exist, largely because we insist on it. When my mother and father began to forget where we lived, what we had done together, and how each of us intermeshed as a family, I understood how wondrous, and needed, the connective tissue of memory is—and I learned, just as dramatically, that where they failed to provide concrete detail, I would interpolate. If I am here, so are they.

All of these essays were published elsewhere. And I especially want to thank Robert Fogarty at the *Antioch Review* for printing five of them and for being such a generous editor. I would also like to thank Michael Koch for publishing three pieces in *Epoch*, which, of course, originates at my university, Cornell. He, too, has been a godsend. Four of these essays were listed as "Notable Essays" in *The Best American Essay* volumes, so I may have done something right.

If anything, my parents taught me the value of love and witness. My parents, whatever their foibles, loved me—and it was a great love, a messy love, an overabundant love. Few people have suffered from an excess of love; millions, in the world, have perished from the lack of it. If these essays are generous, it is simply my parents' gift returned.

In this dark time of war and human perfidy, to be loved is an awesome thing. I have been blessed with many friends who

3

have taken me seriously and who have honored my often abject lack of normal human intercourse. To my distress I did not collect my mother's ashes from the funeral home until three years after her death. I simply left her remains there, as if they were wheat chaff. To this day, I sing the praises of the honorable mortician who—when confronted with my wife and me—simply offered his great unstinting solace. His generosity was an act of near-Augustinian forbearance.

Of course, there were good reasons for my departure from good taste. My mother's illness had removed her from me, well before the flesh had perished. But it is just as truthful to state that I am a very odd person, whose abhorrence of civic decorum, sadly, is often profound.

As James Baldwin reminds us, we all travel down the same streets, however extraordinary they appear to us. Yet I hope, in this small volume, among the commonplace, I may invest the world with a particular taint, a peculiar angling. If these essays are at times ungainly, I hope they are always honest. If they are not, then I have done something inexcusable, for I have failed to honor family, history, and the *sacred* act of human witness.

Yet above all else, I dedicate this book to my wife, Rochelle, who makes me know—in word and quiet gesture—that mercy, tenderness, and hope exist.

I am now fifty-seven years old, and I have never imagined myself as a hopeless romantic, but I am. And how sweet, in this dark time, to feel the wind sweep through the willow, my lovely wife near me.

June 1, 2008
Ithaca, New York

Shadow Boxing

For my father

At age seventy-nine, my father has a remarkable way of remembering things. In his full-blooded narratives, he is often dutifully beating up someone who has been unfair to my mother, has threatened my sister, or has been contemptuous of someone—or something—he deems worthy of his protection. These stories are *glorious* in their intricacies, the delicious how and why buttressing the fateful moment when my father "knocked the man's teeth out," or "broke his jaw," or "wrestled him to his knees."

My father has always told good stories, since he delights in the heroic and loves the way an expectation can bedevil an outcome. In the past, of course, these stories were more *earthly*—that is, most of the tales were true: one could believe the bone, though the gristle, perhaps, was porous. Still, then as now, when my father becomes truly animated, he is often brought to his full standing height, his hands purposeful, free-floating, before he settles back—a bemused, contented look on his face. At this moment, no one could be more pleased with himself. And yet, no matter how wonderful my father's pugilistic yarns, none of these events ever took place. Once, many years ago, my father did hit someone, but that was in the most extraordinary of circumstances. He could have punched others; he is certainly strong enough. But he, by nature and temperament, is not combative.

Like most of us, my father is fundamentally decent and principled. His recent fantasies underscore his pain, although the rest—the blood and fisticuffs—is pure invention. For, above all else, my father is simply relating what he felt in a particular situation, that he wanted to act, and that had he been someone else, fists would fly. And considering the magnitude of the gore amassed in his recent stories, it is a good thing, for had my father pummeled everyone at his exponentially growing rate of recollection, there would not be anyone in Harlem, or in New York City, for that matter, who still possessed his original pearly whites.

In actuality, my father is remarkable for his generosity and lack of bitterness. Although he struggled against much racial prejudice, he remained doggedly optimistic, which is why, I imagine, he was able to become a successful African American physician in a terribly difficult time. He, to this day, is pleased with his life, whatever its involvements and misfortunes—and they have been many, the death of an alcoholic son, the intimate challenge of parenting a brain-damaged daughter, and the loss of his wife of fifty-seven years to Alzheimer's disease.

During his youth in Boston, Massachusetts, in the 1920s, my father attended public schools controlled by the Irish, many of whom had little use for him or his family. Often, his classmates would call him names: few, if any, ever spoke to him. At times, my father thought his middle name was "Nigger." In fact, he was not initially permitted to graduate from his high school, although he was a brilliant student, because the principal would not sign his graduation release form. Though mild-mannered, my father believed in himself; he did not take nonsense from anyone. Proud to be black, he felt—as did his father before him—that he was as good as anyone else, which made him, in the principal's words, "an uppity nigger." Indeed, my father was "paper certified" only after my grandfather's threat of a legal suit, his degree coming to him six months late.

Then, four years later, after my father had graduated Phi Beta Kappa, in three years, from Boston University's College of Liberal Arts, he was admitted to Boston University's College of Medicine but only after the most tortuous of journeys. At the time, no Boston medical school would accept black students, and my father, as the child of a poor minister, could ill afford to go elsewhere. To insure their subterfuge—which depended upon their unanimity—the Boston medical schools (Harvard, Tufts, and Boston University) had a "gentlemen's agreement" whereby they would collectively direct all their black applicants to black medical schools in the South. Yet, as is so often the case in the machinations of those who are truly despicable—those who, in Albert Camus's phrase, wish to be "innocent murderers"—the Boston medical schools could effectively neutralize these unwanted potential doctors through bureaucratic sleight of hand; in reality, these applications were never officially reviewed. Black applicants were not "refused" at Harvard; they were "referred" to Howard. All the poor "successful" applicants knew was that, in a few months' time, they were offered admission to a school to which they had not applied.

For a year, my father remained in limbo. Then, after much intrigue—and with the great help of Dr. Solomon

Carter Fuller, a distinguished African neurologist—my father inveigled an interview at Boston University's College of Medicine. It was an astonishing encounter, to say the least. The medical school's faculty literally looked my father over, trying, one surmises, to ascertain if he were "too black" to trouble the white patients, a consideration not unusual in those days. Indeed, my father wonderfully recounts how the distinguished physicians all huddled around the door of the Boston University Hospital like prairie dogs, as my father, albeit timidly, moved through them on his way to the admissions interview. No one spoke to my father; the doctors simply shot him quick glances as they "busied themselves," trying en masse to enter the elevator before he discerned their enterprise. My father, of course, was not fooled.

Still, one can well imagine these bespectacled gentlemen all gathered in the small lobby, trying to look inconspicuous. And to this day, my father heartily laughs when he details the actions of the chairperson of the admissions committee who made the mistake of dropping his keys in the hospital's lobby. My father naturally picked them up, presented them to the doctor, and was suitably thanked. Yet, it was quite a day for that hapless doctor when, lo and behold, he had to lead the questioning of a young man whom he—and the others—had ostensibly never met before. The doctor never mentioned their exchange in the lobby; my father, of course, remained silent. And in two days, to the astonishment of many, my father was admitted, with little fanfare, to the School of Medicine, the first black accepted in twenty-five years.

Yet in the 1960s, it was not my father but his children who were angry. I saw my father's hurt; I wanted retribution. My father simply believed in being a good doctor, a good provider, and a decent man. The problems he had with Columbia Presbyterian Hospital, the fact that he was the only physician without private patient privileges and the ability to admit his own charges, under his own name, was certainly discussed, but it was not the focus of his life. My father was more interested in his patients and their unusual ailments, treating the legion who couldn't pay. Nothing was more important to him than getting a diagnosis correct—in his office he treated leprosy and, amazingly, identified one of the rarest diseases in the world (a strain of hyperthyroidism), one of the twenty-five cases then listed in the medical literature. Nothing was more crucial to him than providing black people with the best care imaginable, and nothing dwarfed his monumental love for my mother, my sister, my brother, and me.

When I was young, it was rare for me to see my father: he worked from nine in the morning till nine at night, six days a week. But on Sunday—the week's grandest day—the entire family would take the Staten Island Ferry across and back, which is still one of the most magical rides in the world, no matter how many miles I travel and how many wonderful places I visit. My father would always remember that my brother, Paul, loved licorice; my sister, Adrienne, a chocolate milk shake; my mother, a short, small remembrance—a piece of taffy or a bright red kerchief; and I, cashews.

In a phrase, my father was a gentle man, but he was not soft. I recall when I was seven and he and I had gone down to Macy's department store in lower Manhattan. At that time, few black people frequented the most elegant stores: black people rarely worked in midtown; they certainly were not warmly encouraged to visit. Macy's, Saks, and the others were *exclusive*, which inevitably meant, in our national doublespeak, that blacks were not wanted.

Nevertheless, we both had traveled downtown from our Harlem brownstone to purchase a radio for my mother's birthday. I remember how proud I was of our selection; we bought my mother a large cathedral-shaped radio, with eye-catching, globe-like dials. When we entered the elevator, I carried the enormous radio, which was a real treat for me, small and determined as I was. And then we began the slow, three-floor descent through the perfumes, the hand-stuffs, and, finally, to the lobby, which opened like an irrepressible, garish mouth. That day, we shared the elevator with five white men and one white woman, all of whom possessed that studied nonchalance that one perfects in cities. Rule of thumb: one never looks as if one notices anything; one, however, can tell you everything about one's environment, from the size of the man to your left, to the price of his not-so-new raincoat.

Suddenly, as if possessed, the white woman began yelling at my father, and slapped him in the face, screaming that he had pinched her. The elevator was in chaos: the white men and I had not seen anything. Yet I knew that my father would never fondle any woman; he respected my mother far too much to participate in any such odiousness. But then, with no hesitation, my father took his hand and slapped the woman across the mouth, telling her, in no uncertain terms, that he had not touched her, that she must be crazy, and that he had no intention of being hit by anyone for something he had not done.

Now the elevator was in a panic, the white men demanding that my father apologize. For his part, my father simply glared at them, holding on to me, his eyes reassuring but defiant. I still did not know what had fully transpired, but children, as if by osmosis, understand that this is a cruel world and that their parents—no matter how inexplicably they sometimes act—are all they have to protect them. So I, by instinct, just held close to my father: he would explain everything, as he always had. Then, after what seemed like hours, the elevator hit the ground floor, and my father told the men that he would be willing to fight them, one at a time, if that is what they desired. I still remember him chiding: "Just come on now, since you all are so certain I touched this woman. Come on. I only ask that this be a fair fight."

The white men hesitated. Then my father, now conscious of his power and relishing it, rose to his full six-foot height and kept asking—demanding—one of them to fight, his anger deepening, his voice more and more menacing. Thankfully, no one moved. After a few long moments, my father led me out of the store, and we drove home. He was silent, contemplative, victorious. I was scared, yet proud.

For any black person in this country, there is always the possibility of racial insult and the resulting impetus for rage. My father, like all of us, had patiently tried to construct a universe in which he could live his life without recourse to violence. In fact, I can only recall one other instance when he was driven to a place where good cheer and sensitivity could not save him. It was again in New York City, again in midtown, when we hoped to hail a taxi. Cab drivers in New York rarely stop for blacks; they do not like to go to Harlem, for reasons real and fanciful. Yes, it is true that they are often picked upon; but much of this, I suggest, stems from the fact that so few cabs ever venture to Harlem, and far too many Harlemites have suffered from a cab driver's callous dismissal. There is nothing more insulting—in a world full of insults—than having a cab driver—a hired, public servant—slow down, peer into your face, and race off. I don't know if white people have ever felt the anger and dread of anticipating—or even imagining—one's denial. But it is deadly: it makes one want to die; it makes one ready to kill.

That July day, my father and I were looking for a cab and, finally, one came. My father was wearing his best summer suit—he had just come from the hospital—and I was stifling in my private-school clothes, a rigid blue blazer, tie, and gray pants. We certainly did not look impoverished. My father, I would hazard, probably had more money in his pocket than that cab driver made in a month. And we were—at least in our own eyes—worthy of a cab ride up to our house, no matter where it was located.

The cab driver slowed up, and we began to let ourselves in. Yet as soon as the driver saw that my father was black, he immediately sped off, my father's arm, like something im-material, still stuck in the door. I had never seen my father so angry. He kicked at the cab, trying to break the window, and then—in a very strange yet poignant gesture—my father put his hand into his coat pocket, as if to find a gun. Thankfully, it was an empty act. My father had never owned a gun; guns were anathema to him. And yet at that moment, my father had wanted to send that cabby's brains spiraling across the pavement: he wanted to kill something, anything. That he didn't have a weapon is something for which I am forever grateful.

As I mentioned, of late my father tells stories—some familiar, others not—where he does the noble thing, hitting this or that miscreant. He, to my knowledge, has only struck one person, that absurd woman on the elevator. And yet his stories point to a serious truth. He, like all black people, has been hurt by this country, and those bludgeoned teeth, how-ever imaginary, are testimony to the reality that pain festers. For no matter how honorable my father is, the terrible thing about this world, the terrible thing about America, is that one is often made to hate and to want to *smash* something—be it yourself, your children, or, God forbid, some misbegotten soul who, in a different time and place, might have been your friend.

The Mitchell Movement

All of us, I imagine, recall dreadful moments from our schooling. In my case, I attended a venerable, brutal, all-boys school in New York City which was—and proudly so—the oldest private school in the United States. When I was a student there, the Collegiate School consisted of a large red historic building—with great porticoes and a Dutch-stepped roof—and a newer, more utilitarian structure. Most of the old building housed a church named, seemingly incongruously, the Dutch Reformed Church (and one only wonders what it was *before* the Reformation); the rest was used for office space; the other structure, the newer part, was a rather improbable grey chunk of stone, singularly undistinguished.

Collegiate, of course, had its long-held traditions. Most were innocuous; the others—like its penchant to push students to their limits—could be, and far too often were, sinister. Children did learn there; many, however, paid a great price. No one, at least in the twelve years I was enrolled, was not affected: the best students were thick-skinned; another group graduated somewhat punch-drunk; the rest of us departed with something essential missing: we had been violated, but we did not know by what, or how we might be healed. There was just a big gash in our psyches, ineffably dooming us to chase our severed halves, like cut worms.

The school—and my years there—seems forever a part of my memory, and though I would like to think that this essay will be my last word on this painful subject, I find myself going back to my time spent there—again and again—as one switches one's tongue around a diseased tooth to discover if it still hurts. This, of course, is the writer's lot and joy: that which has most hurt him has, paradoxically, given him his life.

I constantly remember being the only black in my classes, and the time, on the first day of Spanish class—I was in the fourth grade—when the teacher, Mr. Calvacca, asked me, "Would the colored boy in the red jacket read the sentence?" meaning *me*, the "colored boy," who now was as beet red as his vermilion blazer. Or the time the music teacher took one of my classmates, who she claimed was making spitballs, and made him stand before the class, fill a six-ounce cup with his own spittle, and drink it down before our terrified eyes. Not only was this act disgusting, but I shall never forget that thin-boned student, trying to create the ghastly meal that he would soon be called upon to swallow.

There are many more such instances—the beating of a boy in the stomach in the headmaster's office for some minor infraction, the constant dreary verbal bullying—but the result was that never to my knowledge was *any* teacher ever punished for any act of cruelty to his or her charges. The school was a famous one: thousands applied to get accepted; it was the door to Harvard, Heaven, and Respectability; and parents took the school's methods as sacrosanct. Rarely would a parent stick up for his child: my parents scurried to the school when a teacher made a homosexual pass at me in the fifth grade; a famous cartoonist once came to the school to dispel a teacher's notion that his son was "too creative." But these were unusual occasions—as exceptional as finding gold in a neighbor's stream.

Since I was black—and one of the first of two black children in the school's three-hundred-year history—things, of course, grew more complicated. Injustice as I perceived it often flared up Janus-faced. Clearly the place believed certain things, and one could get into trouble for any number of reasons, including laziness, *boyishness,* failure to listen, failure to keep a neat appearance, and so on. But for the black child, in a totally alien environment, everything shimmered with possible associations, imaginings, and repercussions. When a teacher singled me out, I often wasn't certain of my offense, and so the justice imposed always seemed, at least initially, to be capricious. Yet in those few *eternal* seconds, the flood of interrogative disgust, self-recrimination, and plain bewilderment was pure agony. And further, if one was singled out because of his *race* (and how could one know?), or because one had simply been lazy, the punishment, thank God, did *finally* come. Since no one knew what the possible punishments were—and the teachers, as I have suggested, were extraordinary in their often abject inventiveness—the child just took it on the shoulder.

Yet in the fourth grade I, of all the students, got myself into an extreme punishment that lasted a year, happening indeterminately but with certainty, for little apparent reason, and with no sense on my part of what I now perceive as its clear intent and clear system. At that time I had a very messy desk, or at least one that my English teacher, Mr. Mitchell, felt was particularly grievous. Mr. Mitchell was a thin, slight man, who walked in a mannered way, as if he thought that the world might steal his spine. In his classes, he could be solicitous one moment, and then quickly turn malevolent, throwing chalk or an eraser at the hapless miscreant. Most of us were scared of him. Indeed, when he gave the homework assignment to name the "Seven Wonders of the Ancient World," I came in the next day with my own list of seven, never realizing that there *actually* were Seven Ancient Wonders—that is, that one could look them up. Instead, I had made up my own tally, including the Great Pyramids, Stonehenge, and some others, happily getting three of the seven right. But when Mr. Mitchell asked me for my list, instead of receiving the expected commendation, he grew enraged and yelled at me for five minutes, calling me an "idiot" and "stupid," until he thought I would cry. But I resisted; not that I didn't want to cry, but because I would not give in. Then, not getting his desired response, Mr. Mitchell continued his diatribe, it seemed for hours. I recall how I struggled to keep myself together, telling myself that I would not let Mr. Mitchell have his way, no matter how brutally he attacked me or how much I wanted to let the tears run. *I will drive him crazy,* I kept repeating to myself, in the way that children, somehow wondrously, invoke the world's irrefutable dictum: he best survives who refuses to perish.

Finally, thank God, the period was over. But I recall that Mr. Mitchell looked at me wistfully as I left the room, and then, in an apparent change of heart, softly stated, "Please listen better next time."

Indisputably, Mr. Mitchell was unpredictable, and when he first commented on my bedraggled desk, he told me that he wanted it "clean by his next class," which I had the following day. On his request, understandably, I did attempt to bring order to things, putting the papers in a folder, putting the pens, stapler, books, and scissors in their respective places. And on the next day, just at the end of the class discussion of *Julius Caesar,* Mr. Mitchell inspected my desk and was pleased. "Just keep it neat, McClane," he prompted.

However, the next class, things to Mr. Mitchell's way of thinking had eroded, and two minutes before the class was to end, he ran to my desk, turned the whole thing over, and dumped all its innards over the floor. "Clean it up," he yelled, his face red, angry.

Immediately I began getting my things together so that I would have my desk upright before the beginning of Mr. Rodgers's history class, in ten minutes. And how I tried! But when Mr. Rodgers approached, in his dapper Brooks Brothers grey suit and Princeton tie, I was still trying to gather up my pens. He looked at me, humorously at first, and then yelled, "McClane, why is your desk such a mess? Look, you're taking up my class time with this foolishness." And then, seemingly moving to the blackboard, he pivoted around, grabbed my desk, and brutally overturned it, sending everything radiating over the floor like slop thrown to pigs. "McClane, you *are* a slob. At the end of class, before lunch, set your things in order."

On the next day I had Mr. Mitchell again, and because I felt certain that my desk was shipshape when he came to me, again at the end of class, I was anxious but not overly concerned. But then, looking in under the desk's lid, he saw that I had three books resting haphazardly on my papers—clearly not a capital offense, but something I should have known would have been cause for concern. And again, his face turned chameleon-like, from a studied calm to a pall of ready anger, and the desk was upended, its contents—and the telltale books—sent everywhere. "McClane, I am losing patience with you," he simply said and walked out.

Mr. Rodgers, this day, came a touch late so I had been able to get my desk uprighted, although the papers were still a mess, and I had pens sitting like toy soldiers hither and yon.

color

Moving briskly through the class, he went to the board, scribbled a line from George Washington, and began to talk. I felt relieved: this day he would not look at my desk. But then, just after Arthur Soong dazzled us with his superior report on Washington's relationship with the Marquis de Lafayette, Mr. Rodgers paused, seemed to remember something, and then slowly sauntered over to my seat. "McClane, I *know* your desk is in order. So, let's just see." And upon opening the desk top, this time he threw everything out and then, with great flair, uprooted the desk, telling me, "McClane, this is becoming *my* preoccupation. I am getting very tired of this."

In the upcoming weeks I would suffer variations of the desk inspection and overturning, at various intervals, but always at the end of Mr. Mitchell's class and before Mr. Rodgers's. If it had occurred every day, I might have grown inured to it, but because it happened at irregular intervals I could never anticipate it. And just when I sensed that the teacher's attention had traveled elsewhere, that John Arkin's penchant for idle chatter was now the center of derision and teacherly instruction, Mr. Mitchell would swell into a fury, prance towards me like a terrible eagle, and my desktop would be hauled open, everything within it flung against the floor. And then, of course, in a few short minutes, Mr. Rodgers would appear, and my desk, now still in a state of disrepair, would be overturned again.

Later on, I would read about the myth of Sisyphus and learn about every manner of vicious cycle; but in those days I was just a young boy who felt, God knows, that I was at the vortex of an unavoidable process, one in which I would always be ridiculed and harangued. If the teachers were trying to get me to clean my desk, or to teach me the importance of industry and proper comportment (which, I hope, was their larger pursuit), then I guess, at least for them, the ends were justifiable even if the means were cruel. But for me, the whole business suggested that there were things in life that made no

18

sense, that one can get locked in a prison of violence and repeated violence, with no sanctuary for understanding or hope. Clearly, Mr. Mitchell and Mr. Rodgers had connived the scheme to *teach* me something, but in their design that I *could never* get my desk straight, they made me understand—albeit powerfully and mercilessly—that there are forces in the world that are evil and malevolent, that I had encountered, in Anton Chekhov's wonderful phrase, "Something out of the language of childhood."

My twelve years at the Collegiate School contained episodes where I was called "Nigger" and made to understand in numerous ways that I was inadequate—in schoolwork, my desire to be creative, even in my desire to be *black*. Yet nothing better captures the horror of being young, vulnerable, and menaced than those two teachers—seemingly in lockstep—moving briskly to my desk, seizing its contents (which were, I now realize, pieces of my life—*me*) and throwing them furiously across the hard, polished floor.

Teachers

Some years ago I decided to leave my university teaching job in upstate New York to pursue other soon-to-be-discovered interests. I was tired of academia, I feared I had become stale, and I wanted to see if I had the courage—and the imagination—to do something else. If you are constituted as I am, teaching can become terrifying; over time, one's endless self-questioning can grow exponentially while the palliative increasingly shrinks. First, the inquiring student seems a nuisance; then she becomes a force; soon, you open the office door with utter trepidation, the person before you a congress of wants and insufferable challenges. When I chided a favorite student, berating her for bringing me a package full of chocolates, I knew it was time to leave.

Teaching is an honorable profession, but not when it is merely centered on a wounded communicant. Metaphorically, I had become a tributary to my own addled river—sluggish, self-infested, weed-choked. So, like millions before me, I decided to go to the Big City, pitch my soul-weary tent, and try my luck. In a few weeks—and all too quickly—I found myself back in the same groove: on Monday, I was tutoring at a city university; on Tuesday and Wednesday, I was a substitute teacher in an elementary school; on Friday, I was a hall monitor in an exclusive public high school, endlessly wandering the hallways like a doomed Odysseus, checking on the hapless students illegally smoking and necking—undeniably, one of the dreariest jobs in creation.

However much my backsliding, I did enjoy the operator who on Tuesday and Wednesday morning would ring with an opportunity to substitute in this or that public school. Education in America is not merely an institution: it is a universe unto itself. Ritually, I would get dressed, have a cup of coffee, and, after a harrowing experience with a road map and a few missed turns, I would enter a classroom somewhere in Westchester County, invariably in one of the more affluent schools, since they had the money to employ me. The students were usually bright, respectful; most, as you might imagine, were simply trying to get through the day. At times, to my astonishment, I would find myself imaginatively entering into the lives of some of them: there was a first-grader in one of my substitute classes who was the shyest child I had ever met, and she and I somehow made a connection. I still wonder about her reticence: the way her world, even in its smallest announcement, seemed to carry the insurmountable sting of censure, and how she—like someone in a Raphael painting—bore it. But most days I spent babysitting a class of students I knew nothing about, or teaching a play or poem that I, thank goodness, still remembered.

One day I was offered a full-time position at a school for the emotionally disturbed after a student literally vaulted from his desk onto me, causing me to fall backwards into a chair, cutting my lip. I recall his assiduous freefall, how he

21

seemed to loom over me like a demented albatross. And I became a minor high school legend when, as a hall monitor, I asked a group of noisy students congregating outside the door of the guidance counselor's office to move on. The students were wealthy, they understood their rights, and they were not used to being told to do anything, especially by an underling who was—at least to them—merely an employee in a "no-account" job. When I politely implored the students for the umpteenth time to cease congregating, one of them—a thin, mouthy, lawyer-in-training—piped up, "How are you going to make us? You've got no power. You can't hit us because you'll lose your job."

Now, I really wasn't very interested in the job, I cared even less for the insolent students, and so I, in a whirl, grabbed that little biped, hustled him off to a corner, and told him in a quiet Jack Nicholson–like voice, "Listen, since I will lose my job, I might as well do some real damage, say, break a few bones. Do you want to push me?" In a minute, he and his confreres were on their way to study hall, calculus, and Harvard, but not before that unctuous conspirator—in the hearing of his friends—announced that I was the best teacher in the school, trying, I guess, to have the last word, even as he made a tactical retreat. I didn't respond; I was already on the way to the library to check the room passes. I had to make certain that Sue or Kevin had an institutionally sanctioned reason to hunger for a book.

Then one day I received a call from my favorite operator to work at a school for the severely handicapped, students whose IQs were in the low teens, who couldn't talk, who couldn't toilet themselves or use a knife and fork. The operator, almost apologetically, told me how difficult the work was, that few people who substituted in this school ever returned, and that it would be understandable if I didn't wish to accept the assignment. She didn't know that I had a handicapped sister who had lived with my family until I went off to college, and how much I missed her, even if we nearly came to blows, since she and I shared the same insufferable stubbornness. Adrienne had been born with brain damage—after the doctor's slap, she didn't breathe for seven minutes—but she was high functioning. She could talk and even write a little. I relished her telephone call to my home every day. At 5:00 P.M. she would call—always at 5:00—always asking the same questions: When are you coming to visit? When are you coming? When I visited her at her residential home on Martha's Vineyard, it was invariably the same routine. Wearing a big, loose-fitting smock, her dancer's lithe movements startling in a 250-pound frame, Adrienne was ecstatic to see me, her ruddy laugh-claimed face centering on me like a laser. After a bit of small talk, I'd ask her what she wished to eat for lunch, and we would ritualistically go out for Chinese food, where she would have chicken chow mein and beg me to allow her to have dessert, always a certain No. Then, after a few small hours, she'd ask me dismissively when I planned to return. That I had driven 450 miles to see her was of little concern: she had done with me.

And though I was always angered at this—it is not easy to drive hundreds of miles, often in perilous snowy winter, only to find yourself so easily dispensable—I knew I'd be there again. Love is a confession, and the love focused in Adrienne's guileless smile, that fixing of my face as if memory could not contain it, as if her contemplation was history's original breath, would pacify the heart of the most abject. The operator couldn't know any of this, or how desperately I needed to find something meaningful. Yes, it was difficult work, and yes, I would be there the next morning.

At first, the Rye School for the Educationally Challenged looked much like the other places I had visited. Educational institutions—which are designed, interestingly, by only a handful of architects—are usually either mock federal monstrosities or garishly utilitarian, with their touted pragmatism, like a bad skin graft, infecting everything. These schools were successful, one hoped; they are certainly ugly enough. And yet the Rye School was different: it had a campus, for starters. Along with the administration building—a giant, red-brick edifice, where I suppose the checks were cut and the meals were ordered—there was a group of low, wildly painted domed huts, like turtles on fire, which seemed, against the utter banality of everything else, as arresting and placative as a Magritte painting.

When I entered the classroom, I was immediately confronted by a tall student with short black hair, who, like a wondrous angel, quickly embraced me, kissed me, and, holding on seemingly for all his worth, grinned unabashedly, while at the same time making a slight audible hum, like a cat's purr. Rudy would hug everything his hands could touch; he'd attempt to coddle a motorcycle, a ball, a bird, anything that moved, making no distinction as to its size, intent, or danger. Rudy would try to nuzzle a speeding car, a lion, or a meteor. He was a veritable love machine. And yet I also sensed—and this too was undeniable—that Rudy could only exist here. Such a miracle of unbridled passion, with his signature love dance and infectious love rattle, persisted only at our behest. The school could allow him the ball, the bird, and me; and it could, hopefully, keep that doom-laden car, at least for a time, at bay.

Up to this point, I had rarely confronted institutions that I could unequivocally term good. In my prison teaching I routinely entered places that deformed, maimed, and ridiculed; the high school I had attended, however many years ago, taught me to hate myself. In short, I had never seen an institution that celebrated the sanctity—the irrefutable *sacredness*—of anyone, and so the Rye campus was an astonishment.

Rudy was the first child I met that day. There were three others: a small girl, Sarah, with blonde hair and cherubic cheeks; a fragile-looking, solemn boy whom I never got to know well; and a dark-complexioned, heavily concentrated boy, who looked like a fleshy dropped biscuit, named Tony.

The class was taught by a brilliant Englishman, Richard Thornton, who had worked with the profoundly handicapped for ten years and had come to the United States and the Rye campus because of his pioneering work. Richard was a big man, who looked a bit like Oliver Sacks, and although he was not in any way hierarchical, I immediately sensed that he was the teacher and I was the aide. His manner was quiet, reflective; his hands moved slowly and continually, as if he wanted to honor the minutest physiological transactions in each movement. As the operator had this morning, Richard explained to me that none of our charges yet knew how to use a toothbrush, that it might take as much as a year's time to get them to be able to toilet themselves, to go into the bathroom, pull down their pants, use the facilities, and reenter a room—a year, if we were lucky. To get one of our students to use a fork, to say an audible word, was a truly miraculous event.

On the first day, I could little understand what Richard meant. I did sense that I was going to work here as long as he'd have me. I was—at least to my thinking—a wandering substitute no more. Richard did ask that I do one thing. He wanted me to read the students' folders, most important, the one concerning Tony. As a child of the sixties, I initially balked—I guess my face gave me away—and Richard, sensing my momentary hesitation, simply reiterated, "Ken, please, read Tony's file. It's important."

To my thinking, all manila folders are alike: they invariably contain a page with a student's name, family's address, and medical and psychological history. All of my students were living in institutions, were listed as mentally impaired, and yet all of them, to my joy, had something in their folders that made them special: Sarah liked to draw; Tony liked

Beatles records; Matthew seemed to grow anxious when the lights were dimmed. Inevitably, we who make up such folders need to believe that a life, however comprehensible, does not easily fit into compartments. Indeed, it is an ironic (and blessed) testimony to our humanity that we fight—almost instinctively—the formulas we create to delimit ourselves. Tony's file began like all the others, and then in the diagnosis remarks I read: "Homicidal/with sadomasochistic tendencies." Now I almost laughed. That little boy with the Buddha-shaped head and the short hair. Right! Richard or not, I was not going to buy this malarkey. Words, language, tags, I knew the litany. Black people were "promiscuous, stupid"; left-handed people were "conflicted." As an African American I had grown up with such "identifiers" all my life.

In 1913, when my mother was born in Massachusetts, the physician described her as "White" on her birth certificate. Given the difficult relations between the races, I presume the physician, if he had any question at all, opined that my mother would prefer joining the racial clan of the Cabots and the Lowells. Although my mother was very fair-skinned, and although there had been much joking about the fact of her reverse passing, to my mother this false racial identification was particularly painful, since she liked the person (the *colored* person) she was. In fact, just ten years before she died, she was finally able to convince a reluctant Boston city registrar to change her racial designation. I can still recall her stating, "I've been black all my sixty-two years," to a young Boston Brahmin who, if his eyes were any indication, had confronted his own private Hades. Yet, at least for ten glorious years, my mother was—in the state's official eyes—finally herself. Thus, labels have great importance to me. If I trusted Richard, I did not easily trust the folder.

After the morning's work, in which we used puzzles to develop eye and muscle coordination, we were scheduled to take the students to swim at a local pool. The water had a calming effect; it also provided for exercise. After seeing that I had developed a good relationship with the class, Richard asked me to mentor two of the students, Sarah and Tony. With no sense of reproach, Richard asked if I had yet had time to read Tony's file.

Since every change in location involved much physical work for the students, I thought it best to take Tony first to the bus, get him settled, and then return for Sarah, who would remain sitting in the bus shelter. When I sat next to Tony to help him fasten his seat belt, he gallantly extended his hand, and I gracefully accepted it. Slowly, Tony took my hand, looked it over, and then quickly forced it into his mouth, biting my knuckles savagely, until they bled. In all honesty, I wanted to hit the child, as much because of the pain as the embarrassment. I was a new teacher, this was my first day, and I had not the faintest idea what to do. Instinctively, I yelled at Tony, telling him to let my hand go. And then, to my astonishment, he broke out in the most extravagant of smiles, the louder I yelled, the more oceanic his grin. It was terrifying. Still, God knows how, I had maintained control.

Now Sarah—who had politely waited for my return—decided to venture out on her own, her body yawing left and right, like a rudderless boat. I tried to watch Sarah and Tony; I tried to watch the others on the bus. Then, somehow escaping his seat belt and me, Tony flung himself off the seat, careened from the bus, and grabbed Sarah, pushing her into the street, right into the path of an oncoming car. Miraculously, the car swerved onto the grass, missed a complement of other children, and came to a halt.

Again, Tony was smiling; he was having the best of times. Here, with diminished intelligence, was undiminishable chaos. Tony would have maimed Sarah, I had to admit, for no other reason than it animated him: it was fun. By the same token, he would have chewed my hand down to the bone had

27

I not yelled at him. Tony was going to act; it was our duty to stop him. Had he had more intelligence—had he had the intelligence of my students at Cornell—he might have found ways to curb his hungers; or, just as possibly, he might have been more skillful at surrendering to them, becoming, God forbid, a Richard Speck or a Jeffrey Dahmer.

Until this time I had believed that those who performed great evil were not born that way—that it was a quirk in their experience that turned them against themselves and others. I still believe this. And yet now I had confronted someone who was—dare I say it—possibly genetically disposed to do the horrific. Here, as my wife would caution, I am probably overreaching. I can't know what had happened to Tony in his short life—it is possible, indeed, that some horrible happenstance at the institution where he lived for two years before I met him was responsible for his present state. Yet whatever these conjectures, it was now plain that nothing could stop Tony from his death dance. Nothing but an ever-vigilant us.

Sitting there in the bus, I thought about why so much of my understanding has been gleaned from such narrative experiences: why, for example, there always seemed to be an experiential codicil to help explain to me what I most needed to apprehend at a given moment, something that allowed me to face the grim world and to remain, at the same time, hopeful, even romantic. Why, just recently, when I was hit by a drunk driver while I was jogging, the accident breaking my leg and scooping out a fistful of skin, a man, hearing my pained yells, jumped from his house and, without even a thought to his utter nakedness, came to my aid. This Tolstoyan character, this bare-butted cherub, shall always remain with me.

Sitting in that public school bus, thinking of Tony and Sarah, I suddenly see Rudy across the street, breaking into a leisurely trot. I watch him size up the bus, trying to figure out how much love it will take to envelop us all. Presently Tony is quiet, Sarah is safe, and Rudy is trying to force his arms wide enough to gather in everything. Richard is escorting him—Tony is still quiet; Sarah is safe. I watch as Rudy contemplates how to arc his arms even wider, his grin becoming irrepressible, his voice beginning to resonate with its love mantra. *This is the way the world works, Ken:* the voices counterpoised, interspiritual: this is the way the world offers up its teaching, its proverbs. Tony is quiet, Sarah is safe, and Rudy, finally love-satiated, extends his arms like a giant octopus. Later Richard—that great teacher—will ask me to come back the next day, and I will.

A King's Holiday:
A Personal Reminiscence of
Dr. Martin Luther King, Jr.

Injustice anywhere is a threat to justice everywhere. We are caught in an inescapable network of mutuality, tied in a single garment of destiny.

—Dr. Martin Luther King, Jr.

The devil does not rape children: we do.

—James Baldwin

In his famous essay "Reflections on Gandhi," George Orwell argues that "saints should always be judged guilty until they are proven innocent," which makes good sense to me. Rarely have I met a saint, or a would-be saint, who wouldn't have been better off being a plain human being, and I do not mean this facetiously. I, for one, am simply trying to face a certain practical reality: we are not saints. For this reason, I want to place my emphasis on what we as *human beings* can achieve—and it is a great deal. If we sometimes wage wars, maim children, and destroy cities, we also, with some frequency, meet the challenges of famine, poverty, and horror. If this were not the case, I doubt if life could be bearable.

A saint, as George Orwell suggests, is often anti-human: he or she believes in things that though laudatory are often against our species. Too often, under the compulsion of a rigid asceticism or a dogged dogmatism, the saintly inhabit a place dangerously insular: for it is only their absolute disengagement from the world that substantiates and permits their saintly life. Indeed, it is their complete abhorrence of life as it is, and we as we are, which, all too understandably, leads us rarely to trust them.

What life teaches, if anything, is that we are *all* novitiates: there are no givens; there is just the human mind and heart, and the hope that someone, somehow, can extricate some meaning from this often grave senselessness. Mahatma Gandhi, as Orwell reminds us, though arguably the most profound moral presence in the twentieth century, forswore sex for what he believed were sound philosophical reasons; but most of us, thank goodness, are not that *holy*.

Obviously, I do not care much for saints, but I do want to share something about someone who, no matter what the present press maintains, was a *good* human being, which is, in this day and age, the highest plaudit. Like most of us, he was all too human. It is rumored that he ran around with women, which is probably true; it is also alleged that he plagiarized some of his writings, including portions of the famous "Letter from a Birmingham Jail," but this may have been more a function of "the preacherly tradition" and how preachers—as a part of their work—view the obvious compliment of incorporating another's insights. Where I attended church in Harlem, the minister often "sampled" the words of another prominent local preacher in much the same manner as a jazz musician interposes a few delicious bars of "'Round Midnight" while playing "Autumn Sonata." The preacher, like the jazz musician, is not stealing: he is celebrating, extending, and reinterpreting. Fundamentally, his enterprise is not an act of theft but of communion: it reminds us that a good tree springs from well-tended soil. And it is a rehearsal, yet again, of the unassailable truth so often repeated during my Harlem upbringing: "I am in you and you are in me."

In the academy, we rightly prize *individual* work and place a great emphasis on authorship, but in the black community, the struggle to honor the fragile possibilities for mutuality trumps everything. In many ways, this *is* our struggle: to show that we come from somewhere, have a connection to others, and can provide corroboration for those who have undertaken the same journey.

While traveling in the South during the 1920s, the great poet Langston Hughes permitted local political organizations to amend his poems as they saw fit: he challenged them to refashion his lyrics as their political situation demanded. For Hughes, his authorship was not important: the demolition of segregation and lynching were. In town after town, Hughes's poems found new stanzas and import, much as the spirituals during slavery were routinely modified to celebrate the safest route to meet the Underground Railroad. As Elizabeth Davey brilliantly evidences in a yet unpublished thesis, Hughes's relationship to his art was novel: novel *and* quintessentially African American.

Still, whatever one's hesitation, scholarly or not, no preacher could have done better by the words and the liturgy than did Dr. King. If he did "borrow" a few phrases here and there, I feel certain that none of his original benefactors would have been disappointed by what Dr. King wrought by his synthesis.

In 1959, when I was eight, I was fortunate to meet Dr. Martin Luther King when he and his wife, Coretta, came to visit us at our summer cottage on Martha's Vineyard. At thirty-one, Dr. King was one of the most famous people in the world, although, at my tender age, I knew only that he was—in my grandmother's highest accolade—a "great man." Three months before, Dr. King and my father had met on a train traveling from New York to Boston, where my father, like countless others, had introduced himself. That both of them had attended Boston University gave them a great deal to reminisce about: there was much ballyhoo about that narrow, flypaper strip of land flanking the Charles River; my father, I feel certain, told Dr. King about his harrowing fight to gain admittance to the medical school in 1933, when the deans of the three Boston medical schools had a "gentlemen's agreement" that no blacks might attend. My father, I surmise, grew animated, his hands gesticulating like a furious scythe, as he detailed the dean's suggestion that he seek admittance to a "black school," which would entail traveling to the South, should he think of becoming a physician at all. My father, understandably, was livid: he lived in Boston; his father was a poor minister; he could ill afford to go elsewhere. In fact, my father would not get accepted to Boston University until he reapplied two years later, even though he had graduated second in his class from Boston University's College of Liberal Arts, in three years, with a major in chemistry. Dr. King would have known the story—it was the usual tale, told in a million different ways, but inevitably revealing a bottomless sea of bitterness.

In addition, for the past three summers my family had taken numbers of Freedom Riders into our home, providing them with an important two-week respite from the raging civil rights struggle in the South. These valiant kids, many of whom were no older than sixteen, had been nonviolently demonstrating for weeks, confronting maniacal segregationists, Klan members, and misanthropes of every description, as they struggled to integrate stores, lunch counters, and bus stations throughout the South. I recall how they showed us the festering cattle prod burns on their genitals, the inflamed welts on their foreheads, their oft-broken hands. To my brother and me, these were *authentic* heroes; at age six and eight respectively, we, like most children, had done little on the world's stage—and certainly nothing that could rival the courageous selflessness of the Freedom Riders, daily putting one's mind and body in the path of those who, in a diabolic crusade, wished to do them bodily harm. My brother, Paul, and I basked in their conversation—we were always underfoot, pesky beyond measure, lapping up everything. Indeed, my father had to remind us constantly to give our vacationers a break. "They are here for rest. Give them a minute, please," he would implore.

In the South, then, it was "sporting" to beat up black protesters—one bar, in fact, gave a prize for the person who brutalized the most "niggers" in a calendar month. These kids who visited us had been spat upon, kicked in the groin, bludgeoned by iron pipes, and burned by cigarettes; they had been thrown into jails that would frighten the most inveterate prisoner. One of our lodgers told me that when he was arrested, his jailers released a live rattlesnake into his cell to see if "niggers really danced." Another simply could not talk about his experience. Looking at my brother wistfully, he explained that he had a sibling about the same age. And then, his tears flowing freely, he picked my brother up in his arms in a gesture reminiscent of that near-evangelical moment in James Agee's novel *A Death in the Family* when the young boy, Rufus, meets his aged grandmother and speaks into the cavern of her ear, and she, in a paroxysm of joy (and yet with great dignity), grabs him, refusing to let go, her urine, like a wondrous amulet, slowly pooling beneath her seat. Somehow, my brother and I knew not to question this occurrence; somehow, silence rose like a great providential bridge.

Often, as a way of explaining to us how they bore it—and also, I imagine, as a way of making certain that they remained connected to the dour world to which they would all too soon return—they would sing us their freedom anthems, composed, as one person put it, "between sitting, getting beaten, and messing one's pants":

You can talk about me just as much as you please
As long as I can bend my knees.
Oh, Oh Lord. Oh, Oh Lord.
Keep your eyes on the prize.
Oh Lord, Oh Lord.

The Freedom Riders all looked out.
The jail cells opened and they all walked out.
Oh, Oh Lord. Oh, Oh Lord.
Keep your eyes on the prize.
Oh Lord, Oh Lord.

At their invitation, my brother and I would join them, singing as best we could, solemn in our desire to please, happy to be included. Although it was fun, we quickly realized that this sharing of song—and the vulnerability it extracted from us—allowed them, however grudgingly, to trust us. What segregation had done, understandably, was to make them wary. Everything was tinged with danger. Though they enjoyed our house, it must have seemed as if we were from the other side of the world—and to a large degree we were. Our ease was immense; our love and admiration for them was immense, also. But the constant hate and human perfidy had worked its lot. Often these gallant kids, when asked their names, would give us an alias: *I am John. He is John. The little one over there, he, too, is John.* And in this they were right: in this damaged world, where four young girls could be blasted to smithereens for simply being black and praying in their church, nothing could be trusted: we, too, could be agents, provocateurs.

Inexorably, to risk connection is to risk denial; and these adolescents, who had seen so much hate and violence, could not easily let their guard down: it was simply too dangerous. I remember how one young lady poignantly asked us if we knew about the South—which meant, I intuited, did we know about them, and their privations? But before we could answer, she started to smile, telling us, almost believably, that what we had seen on the television—the burning buses, the children mauled by dogs—was an overstatement. "Things aren't that bad," she said. Yet just as her mouth moved, the thick gash on her cheek, received just three days before she came to us, glistened in denial.

This, sadly, is all too often the mandate of the victimized: not only are they required to suffer, but they are also called upon to deny the overwhelmingly incontrovertible. And as I watched her anguished face, I recalled, with particular bitterness, the line from the spiritual: *If I had my way, Delilah, I'd tear this building down.*

Luckily, children—for that is what my brother and I were—are permitted the largesse of wonder and empathy; but even that, alas, sometimes fails. My brother and I were rich compared to our visitors: we had a beautiful house; we didn't worry for anything; we, most certainly, were not overtly menaced. These kids, in truth, had *bled* for us; but most saliently—and it could not be lost on these intrepid visitors— we were *safe*. And safety is expensive: what price we had paid—including, possibly, the repudiation of them—kept them at a great remove, one no less immense than the miles separating our wind-swept ocean from the dust-ridden, blood-clotted roads of their besieged South.

In truth, the only time I was pleased to have any association with my elite private school, and the privilege it afforded me, involved a sullen, big-boned Freedom Rider, John

Griggs—barely sixteen—who had come to visit us. John (again that well-rehearsed name) had been brutally beaten by a Mississippi policeman because he had wanted to sit in the "public" waiting room at a bus station. One of my school classmates, Whit Stillman, who also had a home on the Vineyard, visited while John was with us and told his father, then assistant secretary of commerce in the Kennedy administration, about the savagery of the cattle prod when used on people. Whit had seen the terrible scars on Griggs's body and penis; he, as I, was ashamed that this could happen to anybody in this country; we, with the idealism that only the young can muster, *had* to do something. So, at his son's request, Mr. Stillman relayed his horror to the president, and in a few days, Robert Kennedy introduced litigation immediately barring the use of cattle prods on human beings.

A long cylindrical device, resembling a bike tire pump, the cattle prod consists of batteries and an alternator. The prod, as its name suggests, is effectively used on livestock to get them to go where a farmer wants; the batteries, for a short interlude, can deliver a massive jolt, enough power to move a recalcitrant thick-skinned cow, singe the hair off one's arm, or incapacitate a hapless person for days. In fact, a close friend of ours, William Preston, during a foolhardy civil rights fund-raising demonstration, stuck the prod into his forearm and found that he couldn't move his fingers for a week. In a few seconds, his arm turned a sickly blue, the skin blistered like a molten pizza, and his fingers crimped. Yet the notion that the prod was routinely used on the genitalia of men and women alike encouraged the height of revulsion.

I can't relate how my family survived the anticipation of Dr. King's visit. Suffice it to say that the always sand-filled and damp cottage had be aired and primped, the lawn cut and landscaped, the porch scrubbed and de-mildewed. For the first time in my memory, my mother seemed overjoyed to assume the housework. Unlike the usual terror-ridden days before people were to be entertained, when my brother, sister, and I were always in the way, asking the wrong questions, or simply acting "too cute," these days of sanitizing were sweetened with my mother's humming. Duke Ellington's "I Love the Sunrise," with its beautiful, majestic, operatic accents, was played and replayed. In fact, my father, always the comedian, upon seeing my mother's industry, jocularly volunteered to ask Dr. King to remain indefinitely. And although I did not want to go that far, I did enjoy my mother's *happy* hysteria.

I've recently read that Dr. King's visit to the Vineyard was one of his only two vacations in those five tumultuous years following Rosa Park's legendary refusal to move to the back of the bus. At the time the Southern Christian Leadership Conference (SCLC) was involved in around-the-clock sit-ins, and Dr. King was either getting arrested himself or fulfilling his exhausting lecture schedule—450 lectures that year alone—which provided the all-too-necessary bail funds. As things were, the sit-ins were intensifying, the Old Order was rapidly falling away (albeit with much hate and bloodshed), and the constant money that Dr. King had to produce with his ever-magical oratory—"drawing water from a rock," as his friend Ralph Abernathy playfully termed it—remained the highest priority. Actually, Dr. King had planned to spend a week vacationing on the Vineyard; demands, however, meant that he would only stay two days.

Whenever we stopped our blue Volkswagen bus, I vividly remember how Dr. King was immediately recognized. Everyone knew who he was; many wanted autographs. And as is so often the case in such situations, people found themselves becoming either tongue-tied or loquacious, the words seemingly spawning on their own. Upon seeing Dr. King, one man—nicknamed "Bubbles" for his irrepressible mouth—suddenly became quiet, obsequious; another woman, running across the street in life's greatest transgression, momentarily forgot her three-year-old child. Indeed, it was a delightful cornucopia for someone of my general air of romanticism: Incredibly, the lion here had truly become the lamb.

Interestingly, Dr. King seemed not to notice the pandemonium his appearance caused; he just sat there talking, smiling, and signing autographs, much as if he were at the local storefront in a Norman Rockwell painting. Indeed, I presume his enormous following—his great charisma—centered on his uncanny ability to make everyone feel important and sacred. I could tell that he enjoyed talking to people about their children, their jobs, and their hopes. Dr. King didn't speak much: he *actively* listened. And every once in a while, he would sneak a wonderful, infectious smile.

The people he met sensed that although he might be a "great" man to others, here, with them, he was Martin. And that thought, which really wasn't true—these people had never met him before; they could not say they knew him—seemed nonetheless plausible. And in the face of the largely incontrovertible—and the reality that no one wished to believe otherwise—the need became the man.

After numerous people had met Dr. King, a tall, pretty, cream-colored woman, wearing a bright, billowy, yellow hat, presented herself. Mrs. Lloyd's hat brim was so generous, so extraordinary, it reminded one of the pictures of Saturn's colorful rings, featured in those garish Earth Science textbooks prominent in the late 1950s. As he had done previously with everyone, Dr. King looked at her, asked her name, looked again at her face, and then, as if smacked by a rifle butt, he suddenly faltered. Mrs. Lloyd had merely acted as the others had: she had introduced herself, stated how much she respected Dr. King, and placed a small contribution into his hands for the SCLC. And yet Dr. King was visibly shaken, his hands trembling, his eyes ranging loose and unfocused. I remember looking into my father's face, trying to discover what all this meant, and how my father, also unnerved, did not move.

In a few seconds, Dr. King caught himself and tried desperately to reassure Mrs. Lloyd and the rest of us that he was fine. She, if anything, only sensed that Dr. King had suffered a temporary bout of nausea; the whole commotion was over in an instant. And yet Dr. King spoke to Mrs. Lloyd busily for ten minutes, seemingly clinging to her, as if she were a life raft.

After Mrs. Lloyd had gone, and we began our short ride to the beach, following the long, pretty, sand-swept streets, with their shingled cottages and cupolas, Dr. King explained what had happened. Two years before, during a trip to Harlem to autograph copies of his book *Stride Toward Freedom,* a smartly dressed woman, Izola Curry, burst though the crowd hysterically yelling, "I've finally got you," and quickly jabbed a jade letter opener into Dr. King's chest, plunging the blade a hair's breadth from his aorta. Dr. King survived but only because, as his surgeon stated, "He didn't cough for the three hours while the operation was performed." In her wild yellow hat, Mrs. Lloyd had reminded Dr. King of the lady who had stabbed him; when he saw her, he had felt the letter opener reentering, like something dull but purposeful—and always, as Dr. King stated, "the terrible hate of a woman who didn't even know me."

In Dr. King's attempt to return Mrs. Lloyd's tranquility—and ensure his own—he had talked to her for an extraordinary ten minutes. My father, upon hearing this story, assured Dr. King that Mary Lloyd clearly was not frightened; indeed, as we all noted, she left looking buoyant. Mary had been out on her daily walk to purchase the paper; instead, that day, she had met one of the most important persons in this nation's history.

Relieved, at least for the moment, Dr. King playfully suggested that we should all enjoy "nature's baptism" and savor the ocean. And we did, swimming, hoping the cool Atlantic waters might help him forget—for a few precious seconds—that the world of injustice always beckoned.

On the trip back from the beach, Dr. King asked if we might stop by a florist: he wanted to buy some flowers. On an island the size of Martha's Vineyard, a florist is not a commonplace, but we found one, in a small, picturesque fishing hamlet, where Dr. King purchased an enormous number of white roses, twelve of which he graciously presented to my mother, who still cherishes them. Then, once at our house, Dr. King asked if he might use our telephone; he wanted to call Mrs. Lloyd, explain what had happened during the day, and give her some roses. Learning that she and her husband would be at home that evening, he asked if he might visit them after dinner. At the house, among a number of less important messages, was a telegram for Dr. King: *Bull Connor has arrested another three hundred Freedom Riders. Martin, we need the bail money,* the telegram simply read. And so Dr. King would leave in the morning, barely thirty-six hours from the moment he first began his six-day vacation.

This is certainly not an earth-shaking vignette. After dinner, Dr. King took the flowers to the Lloyds' house and spent two hours explaining what had caused him to appear so fragile that afternoon. What they talked about I do not know; I do know, however, that Mrs. Lloyd will never forget those roses, and the man who cared so much for her feelings that he would spend two precious hours with her. Dr. King's meeting with her, of course, was not historic: he was not conferring with President Kennedy or the Justice Department; no "I Have a Dream" speech would come from the deliberations.

And yet one man understood that one woman deserved an explanation for his possible "assault on her dignity." It was probable, as I suggest, that Mrs. Lloyd did not sense the anxiety that Dr. King ascribed to her: chances are she was too caught up in the throes of her own chance meeting with a personal hero to feel much else. But since Dr. King intuited that she might have felt uncomfortable or "remotely vexed," it was his obligation to set things right. This action, though not saintly, was the result of one man appreciating that each of us has an obligation to the other, no matter how small or transitory the appearance of our slight. Dr. King—though all too human—was doing best what only human beings could: he was risking connection, demanding it. This love, so human-centered as to be near inassimilable, is not the stuff of measure, orthodoxy, confinement, or rule: human beings, if lucky, may find it; *human* beings, I repeat, if lucky, may find it.

Color

For my mother

In 1977, when my mother was in her early sixties, she needed to produce her birth certificate to apply for Medicaid, a rite of passage fraught with enormous trepidation, especially for someone of my mother's near-ecumenical disengagement: she simply would not entertain any act of bureaucracy or officialdom; irreproachably the artist she was, my mother kept her mind uncluttered with those things she deemed immaterial. She would pay the paper lady, because everyone needed money, and she admired the woman's truculence; yet she would never pay the water bill or the real estate taxes— and it was not simply that my father handled that; things were never *that* simple. It was that these commitments were beyond her compass, as cut off from her world as marzipan and a mongoose. And as you might expect, in her cooking, too, there was a discreet inattention: when she would remember to include all the ingredients, she would make a splendid spaghetti; at other times, there would be a wonderfully restrained sauce, "spaghetti imaginara," I used to call it, which would involve a slight tossing of cloves and peppers, and a faint sprit of tomato. Sometimes, in all honesty, these creations were quite marvelous: the loss of one staple, overshadowed by the pungency of another; and sometimes, with my mother's fullest approbation, it was good that we lived in close proximity to two Chinese takeouts.

Surprisingly, my mother had never been asked for her birth certificate in sixty-two years, and its whereabouts were, to put it kindly, obscure. Finally, after a flurry of scouring every possible inch in our Harlem home, even descending into her favorite hideaway, the not-to-be-touched window seat box, with its tangles of papers, my mother conceded that it had been lost. So, with little fanfare, she dutifully sent off a request for a duplicate to Boston, Massachusetts, where she had been born, and it came in the mail in a few days. My mother, as was her wont, didn't open the letter for a week: it sat out on the library table, with the unread *Crisis* magazine, the AARP bulletin, and a few advertisements.

But one day, after my father had come home early from the office, my mother opened the letter, and I overheard her tell him, with much force, "There must be a mistake; *we* have to do something; we'll take a trip." My mother was being characteristically theatrical, since she used to do summer repertory, but this was not her intention: she was merely reverting to a past life, where the world had made sense to her, a time in which she had acted with Eli Wallach and Anne Jackson, thrilling the summer residents of Martha's Vineyard with weighty theatrical fare, including *Five Take Away Two* and *The Little Foxes,* a play that caused its author, Lillian Hellman—who lived on the island and attended the opening night performance—to upbraid my parents brutally for changing the word "nigger" to "Negro," in my first encounter with the intricacies of authorial intent versus the wishes of a custodial community. Ms. Hellman, though formidable, lost the argument: she threatened to sue to stop the play, but Dashiell Hammett, her paramour, like a provident voice from offstage, pronounced, "Lillian, this play *is* about language—this is the world: *these* people." Mr. Hammett was speaking about my mother and the others, most of whom, though mediocre actors, were heroic participants in the civil rights struggle then overtaking the country. There was Dr. David Spain, the clinical pathologist, who performed the autopsies on the slain civil rights workers Schwerner, Goodman, and Chaney in Mississippi, at great personal peril; Kivie Kaplan, national president of the NAACP, who would give everyone a "Keep Smiling" card, two decades before the button craze, at a time when the world seemed bereft of anything humorous, with the seemingly omnipresent litany of dead civil rights workers, the endless legal battles, the country mired in obfuscation, nullification, and perfidy; and Bill Preston, who, in a foolhardy attempt to dramatize how the cattle prod could be used by segregationist police to "immobilize" a part of the body, stuck the small cylinder-shaped generator into his arm, and watched his fingers turn a sickly mauve, his arm as hapless as an ice cube in Saudi Arabia. These were the *true* actors, Hammett reminded Hellman. "Get off your high horse, Lillian," he said, winking at her.

Suddenly, my mother used the expletive, "Damn," with a sense of vitriol unknown to me, her hand clutching the opened letter, the birth certificate. Although my mother could make a look an omen, she never used profanity. This day my father was quiet, his entire bearing as quiescent as slag water: he had patients to see and hospital rounds to make. From his tepid response, I could tell that my mother's angst would not concern him, at least not in a physical way. And I could tell, just as powerfully, that my mother was not to be deterred. I was home from college, I heard my mother offer: I'd take a few days off, *we'd* settle this thing. My mother had rightfully perceived that my father, though compassionate, was sliding off center: like an underpowered tractor, he meant to take the crest of the hill, but it would not happen, in this world or the next. For my part, I hadn't yet learned how to dodge my mother's gargantuan enthusiasms; I hadn't, in all honesty, ever wanted to. Still, I'd never seen my mother so discombobulated.

As was the case with many people, my mother (neé Dora Genevieve Greene) had been born at home, in 1913, in Dorchester, Massachusetts, a suburb of Boston. The physician had come to her house, helped in the delivery, identified her gender, and specified her race. As her mother, my mother was very light-skinned—"lemony," as some in the black community term it—and the doctor, with dispatch, assumed that she was white. Although located in the North, Boston was hardly the cradle of egalitarianism its Founders celebrated. The doctor, like my mother, lived in a world where color defined, and he followed its dictates. He presumed—and one could easily see why—that my mother *had* to be white. And even if she were possibly not, the consequences of which he could barely imagine, wouldn't she prefer to cast her fate with the Cabots and the Lowells, those who had the fine mansions on Beacon Hill? For his part, the doctor didn't wish to trouble my grandmother, who was vexed enough after the long delivery. And why would he dare to question her heritage and pedigree—for she certainly *looked* white—in a town and nation where race was the harbinger of all that life offered? No, it was clearly better to be white, the doctor reasoned. And so my mother was white. Plain and simple.

And, in truth, my mother could easily be seen as Caucasian, if one did not know that black people are often olive-skinned, and that many of us in this country, however we may try to hide it, have been blessed by the Nile and the Thames. For black people of my generation, it's a private joke (albeit a grisly one) to infer who in fact may be black: some people are clearly passing, and they often suggest to you, almost subliminally, that you shouldn't turn them in; others—through the various intrigues and circumlocutions of fate—have never been made to confront the resonant sting of the tar bush, which, though no less problematic, still incurs my awe and sympathy. In questions of race, one can get both angry and saddened at the same time. It is not pleasant to confront someone who sees your racial life as trivial or immaterial, even should that disregard be based on guilelessness or ineptitude; still, no one wishes to see a person of color, however misguided, hurt.

I must state here, as my wife reminds me, that I am dangerously limited by my own experience. Race for me is the Rosetta stone—it informs everything, and is the landscape, if you will, by which all my determinations are made. Those younger than I, those in the after–"I Have a Dream" generation, see their lives differently: they believe, or at least some of them maintain, that race is simply one of the ingredients in their self-orchestrated, bouillabaisse identity. For me, if I can carry the metaphor a bit further, the pioneering chef is far less the determinant: I'm not sanguine about my ability as an epicure, nor has the world, at least in my experience, proved otherwise. Although I do know that the world has changed, that the terrors that challenged my parents were of a vastly different order from those I now confront, I also know that I have been called "nigger," that people have questioned my right to frequent certain establishments, and that I still remain a "problem" for many of my countrymen, as the omnidurent affirmative action debate ever affirms. Although I am less in danger of being bludgeoned by pipes and burned by cattle prods, I have encountered, and far too often, that overlong, dreary glance, which, under the thinnest of pretexts, confirms me as a probable thief or rapist, and hurls me out of the sanctuary.

And yet to be honest, much of my race consciousness stems from my parents' lives, where race was the essential calculus. When I was young, everyone mentioned the race of those with whom they met. When we talked about black people, one's race was usually invoked simply as an indication that the person was *not* white. But when we talked about white people, the mention of race implied something far more mysterious, unruly, and in need of definition: whiteness, since it was so much a force in our life, and often a negative one, had to be delimited, as if we were talking about a natural phenomenon, which, like the wind, could be a slight winnowing or a mighty hurricane. I well recall the proverbial, "Bill Preston, you know the white guy who helped with fund-raising for the NAACP, he really brought in a great deal of money." Or, "Millie Cohen, the pretty white woman who took in the Freedom Riders, she was fearsome for being so short." The articulation of race here was meant to suggest difference positively, to place this person in context and against all other inferences. In my parents' generation, most white people, sadly, were not Bill Prestons or Millie Cohens: they were not pioneers or revolutionaries. They were simply human beings, inspirited by fears, exhortations, the tentative joy of a baby's first step, and the often far too powerful sorrowings of this world.

And yet there were good white people. When my father was set to graduate from medical school in 1939, the first black to earn a degree from a Boston medical school in thirty years, he initially could not attend his graduation banquet since the Boston hotel it was to be held in was segregated, and blacks and Jews were not welcomed. But when my father's best friend, the only Jewish student in his class, told his parents that my father and he were barred from the festivities, his parents bought the hotel, in a flurry of entrepreneurial aplomb hard to imagine. On the night of the banquet, the hotel proudly proclaimed: "Congratulations to the class of 1939. We are under *new* management. *Everyone* is welcome, everyone." Or I well recall when my parents wanted to buy a house on Martha's Vineyard in 1941, when the island was a lovely, unknown atoll. My father had "discovered" the island in the most unusual manner. At age fourteen, escaping his minister father and his "difficult" mother, my father had shipped out on an oceangoing tug, with nary a word to his family, and plied the coast from New York harbor to Nova Scotia, working as a steward. In very rough seas off the Elizabethan Islands, his tug foundered, and he and the crew spent ten days on the Vineyard during the inquest. In later years, my father would always refer to Martha's Vineyard as "God's lifeboat," although as he became older, and the Calvinism leached out of him, the religious imprecations of this utterance impelled him simply to term the island: "Magical."

Initially, no one would sell my parents a home in other than the small black community on the island. Like Boston, Martha's Vineyard was teeming with prejudice. The homes sold by realtors to blacks were small, shack-like, and dreary. My parents wanted a house with a view, a large porch, and some land, and they had the money. Finally, after seeing a covey of less than helpful realtors, my parents came upon the office of one Homer T. Bodfish, which is not a contrived name.

Mr. Bodfish was a thin, wiry man, whose only physical movements were ones of great consequence, as if his very physiology was anchored to the Earth's axis. When my parents knocked on his door, he initially waved them off, saying, "I've made enough money today. Go away." But my parents would not be deterred.

Finally, Mr. Bodfish let them in, and my father told him about my family's desire to purchase property on the Vineyard—good property, property that Mr. Bodfish himself might like to own. Saying nothing, Mr. Bodfish looked them over, and then pointed to a massive stack of newspapers, balanced like an adroit seal. They were Father Divine missives, full of the prophet's tracts on religion, one's responsibility towards others, and racial harmony. Father Divine had created large interracial congregations across the country, full of people who would do anything for the prophet. At some eating places run by the faithful, a chair remained always at the ready for "Father" should he arrive. Mr. Bodfish asked my parents if they knew of Father Divine, and my parents disclosed how much they valued Father's service. Father Divine's minions often acted as hospice workers for my father's patients. For a mere dollar a day, they would nurse a bedridden patient dawn till dusk. My parents must have said the right thing, because Mr. Bodfish volunteered, "I'll show you *one* house. If you don't want it, that's it. One house. Come tomorrow." And then he rose dismissively, his body moving as if it were one lean piston.

My parents bought that "Divine" house—it was designed by Thomas Goethals, the architect of the Panama Canal, and it was truly gorgeous, with a three-hundred-foot porch, a palatial sunroom, and a view of Oak Bluffs harbor, which is one of the loveliest vistas on the island. Interestingly, the neighbors took a long time to warm to my parents, and I use the word "warm," as you will soon understand, with a slight snicker. Incredibly, one family literally moved their house away—three weeks before my parents were set to move in, they were confronted with a massive gash in the countryside; the house, like the omnipresent Vineyard fog, had mysteriously scampered off. Less original, the other "Yankee" neighbors simply kept their stony distance, and one understood why, as a friend admonished me, "they could burn witches" here.

In truth, rarely, if ever, did anyone ever speak to anyone in my family, with the exception of my sister who was, to put it mildly, irrepressible. With her boundless wanderlust and her uncontainable gaiety, even the stoic New Englanders could ill contain themselves. But with my parents and me, the neighbors continued to act as if we were an infestation of locusts—if they waited long enough, we would surely disappear. Then, early one July morning, a young woman knocked on the door, and in the finest of New England accents, offered: "Excuse me, *excuse* me, your house is on fire," and indeed it was. As a result of its ancient electrical wiring, the back of the house was completely aflame, blazing as if it were a husk of dry wheat. My father, since he *too* was a New Englander, offered a hearty "Thank you," with that laconic impassivity that must be genetically encoded.

Although we lost the toolshed, a few trees, and a ratty bathroom, no one was injured: the fire was, in actuality, more smoke than ash. Irrefutably, after that episode, which must have impressed everyone with its utter absurdity, it seemed as if we had wheedled ourselves into the community. Suddenly, the voices opened, and the houses became welcome way stations for palaver, on the slow walk downtown. Incredibly, we'd never known so many people lived beside us.

Still, of course, there was the omnipresent litany of racial denials, denigrations, and humiliations that continued to confront my parents. In 1942, during the Second World War, my father offered to enlist in the Army as a physician to aid in the war effort. He knew that men were dying in Europe, and he wanted to help. But because the Army medical corps was all white, they did not need his services. At the time, he received a very curt note, thanking him for his interest, but telling him that the hour was inauspicious. Then, a year later, after the number of maimed and dying doughboys had skyrocketed, two officers came to my father's office to beseech him to join the military. My father declined. As he told them, "If I wasn't good enough for you twelve months ago, I'm not interested now." The Army, now desperate for doctors, threatened to prosecute; my father remained adamant. During the war, he did treat patients sent stateside: he was a patriot, but he wouldn't enter the Army. "They'd have to threaten my children for me to go," he said, many years later. "I was a doctor then, I'm a doctor now, screw them."

"Ken, we've got to travel to Boston and get this thing corrected," my mother said, as we began our mother-son sojourn. And so we left Harlem, drove across the 155th Street Bridge, crossed beyond Yankee Stadium and the projects located on the old Ebbet's Field, where I had seen Willie Mays hit towering home runs, and traveled up the Saw Mill Parkway, that lyrical road that snakes along the Hudson, much as it did when it was a nineteenth-century carriage path, gamboling through the low fields and the omnipresent willow trees. This route had always been my family's favorite—although slow and torturous, it was beautiful, and it honored my parents' love for the elegiac. As I recall, my mother was dressed cunningly: she was very beautiful, with a complexion like Dorothy Dandridge, and one could see the marriage of the Indian, the Portuguese, and the African in her high cheekbones. Her hair was now white; years before, it had been long, often pulled back. But this day, she reminded me of Janie in Zora Neale Hurston's magnificent novel *Their Eyes Were Watching God*. There was tremendous authority in her presentation, and yet she maintained, and how gloriously, the aura of the child, with no hint of the stony ingénue.

The Boston Bureau of Statistics is located near the Boston Commons—and it was sobering to pass the graves of those who had fought in the Revolution, to see the statue of Crispus Attucks, a black man, the first person to die in the American Revolution, and to see the white dead so neatly packed together, as if they were, in some inadvertent way, mimicking the slave ships with their horrific holds. *That there was hardly room 'tween-decks for half the sweltering . . . stowed spoon-fashion there; that some went mad and tore their flesh . . .* , writes Robert Hayden in his poem, "Middle Passage."

Still, Boston remains an irrefutably consequential place for me to visit. My parents were born there and lived there until they came to New York and had me, which affirms, obviously, that before I was born they had a life, awash in mystery: and it is always incredible to think of the world before you were present, to think of your parents as somehow free, as individuals, as having a history unencumbered by the history *you* represent. And yet I've never spent more than a few days in Beantown. Often regaled as the center for America's ethical values, the city seems the most garish of absurdities to me, given my past. Whatever the attractions of Boston, the U.S. Constitution, Bunker Hill, Faneuil Hall, and Paul Revere's workshop, my family's life there was brutally circumscribed by race, and my father was always fighting. In high school, he was told that he shouldn't think of college: the unskilled trades were for him. When he took geometry—since he *was* going to college—the teacher, who happened to be Irish, failed him even though he had done brilliant work. The teacher didn't even grade his exam: he simply put down a big F. When my father was forced to retake geometry in summer school, he never opened a book in preparation. When he sat for the exam, he scored a perfect 100. Amazingly, when a number of his white classmates failed to pass that summer, he was asked by the examiner to take a lower grade, thereby altering the curve, and allowing the others to inch by, something which my father magnanimously did.

When my father decided to become a physician in 1935, he applied to the three Boston medical schools—Harvard, Boston University, and Tufts—and all of them denied him entrance, even though he had graduated from Boston University's College of Liberal Arts, second in his class, in three years, with a major in chemistry. In those years, none of the Boston medical schools would accept black students; incredibly, my father was told in an interview that should he be accepted to Harvard, he would have to transfer after two years and graduate from a different medical school, one "more fitting" for my father's talents. The Harvard Dean of Admissions—an unreformed Southerner—was not going to permit a black Harvard doctor, not on his watch. Still the inveterate hardhead, my father persisted in applying to the three schools, knowing that his chances were dim.

In April, when others learned about their medical school prospects, my father received no official response from any of the institutions; there was no thin or fat envelope, chilling or animating his enthusiasm. Neither declined, accepted, or wait-listed, my father's application was simply mired in eternal stasis, resting, he imagined, on some functionary's desk, until America ceased to be a Republic. Finally, after a wave of letters, and an ultimate rejection, my father accepted the incontrovertible: he was not going to medical school in Boston, at least that year.

Luckily, after a year teaching English in Pennsylvania, my father reapplied to Boston University and was finally admitted, where he graduated among the top three students in his medical school class. As a prerequisite of his admission, however, he was told that should any white patient object to being assigned to a black physician, he was willingly to let the patient be transferred. And though my father understandably bristled at this suggestion, he wanted to be a doctor.

Still, there were some humorous moments in his medical school career, albeit bitter ones. My father heartily laughs when he recollects the time he confronted a white mental patient on his ward. The patient, who was clearly manic, took one look at my father, stuck out his tongue, rolled his eyes, and hollered, "Oh, a nigger!" My father's ambivalent delight here, I suspect, hails from his incredible sense of displacement. As the madman understood, my father was the outrigger, the outcast, the lowest of the low; this pitiable fool—like all his literary forebears—spoke all too discerningly, embodying, in his abject certitude, the absolute, bone-numbing desperation of my father's predicament.

54

At home, in Boston, things were little better for my father's family. When my grandfather, the minister, walked daily to his Episcopal parish, passing through South Boston, he was often racially taunted and spat upon by the neighborhood hooligans. After a particularly galling spitting spate that endured for weeks, my grandfather came home and told his four sons that God, in his eternal goodness, had *finally* provided, since no one had spat at him in five days. Walter, the oldest of my grandfather's boys, quickly reaffirmed his father's belief that "God was wonderful," neglecting to tell his father that his sons, as God's emissaries, had punched numerous white boys in the mouth that spitless week. And Walter, too, had his contretemps. Since Walter was very light-skinned, with a mild resemblance to Charles Lindbergh, he was often mistaken for white. When one of the white girls in his class took a fancy to him, Walter was told in no uncertain terms by a teacher that he was not to take this girl out. Yet Walter did what he desired, in matters of love and lust. And suddenly his grades started to slip. Once his race became a matter of contention, his intelligence, lo and behold, began to falter.

"How can I help you?" the registrar boldly asked my mother and me. He was in his mid-fifties, wearing a blue suit and a conservative tie, and approached us with a warm, albeit reserved manner.

"Sir, we have a problem, hopefully not a big one," my mother replied. I watched as my mother calculated how much time she had, what the nature of her audience was, and how her presentation might work to best effect. "Well, sir, I recently had need of my birth certificate and found out to my dismay that it contained an error concerning my race, which was listed as 'white.' Now I know this may seem like a small matter to you, but to me it's essential. Sir, I've been black all my sixty-two years, and I'm proud of that. I've grown three children, helped my husband attend medical school, and faced many things—all as a *black* person." She waited, allowing it to sink in. "Sir, can the race be changed to black?"

I watched the registrar as he tried to remain imperturbable, his face congealing, as if nothing had ever roiled beneath its surface. I could sense that he was hoping that the Registry procedures, if he could simply recall them, might proffer some guidance to handle this wild woman with her strange request.

My mother, too, had seen his remote apprehension: she knew it was time to employ all her skills, before he closed the door. This was the moment she had always relished in her acting career—the zero hour, when a good performance, if it were to be, must sally forth. If he wasn't moved by my mother's confession, his veins were filled with quicksilver, and nothing could make the dead bones live.

"My children have always been told to be proud of their race. It was important to me and to my husband that they be fair to others, but that they also know who they were and whence they came," she said. "I'm black. My parents were black. I've been black as far back as I can trace. Can you change what is clearly an *injustice*?"

The word seemed to hang in the air like the airship Hindenburg before it crashed to the ground. I felt that my mother knew what she had done, how she had unleashed, like the grandest confection, something which returned us to the original, the preconceived, the preordained. It was as if we hadn't yet read Freud, or known about Abraham Lincoln, or Dr. Martin Luther King. The word "injustice" simply sat there, molting, as if we were present at the creation of the firmament.

The registrar sensed his newfound station, even if he didn't know how to shoulder it, and I felt innately sorry for him. He was a good man, but he was not a visionary one: the job he held was ideally suited for him, its contours met his enthusiasms, and he, like most of us, had become limited by its small buffetings, abandonings, and silencings.

After a while, the registrar simply said, almost inaudibly, "Mrs. McClane, this is a legal document. I understand you're concerned, but *I* can't do anything. It's a legal document of record."

My mother thanked him, seemingly convinced of her failure. But after we left the building, she told me, "We'll come back tomorrow. There'll be another registrar. I'll convince him or her."

The next day, my mother was ebullient. Amazingly, my mother had not discussed the previous day's denial: at dinner we talked about my cousins; after dinner, we talked about Cape Cod, and our hope for a quiet, uneventful summer. In fact, it seemed as if my mother had completely relegated the day's comings and goings to some place beyond her interest; wherever it was, it held no sway now. Yet I was completely caught in the present, in my imaginings. In the best instance, we would go to the Registry, my mother would work her magic, and a black Mrs. McClane would prevail; in the worst scenario, we would undergo a thousand small-notioned bureaucrats, and I would never leave Boston. This, too, seemed a distinct possibility.

The next morning, the bright day seemed to match my mother's high spirits, and I almost found myself believing that the world would hear us. But there had been other bright days: my brother had died of alcoholism on a crisp blue morning, and so I was, to be truthful, as directed and as directionless as a butterfly.

The new registrar was young, with the faintest trace of stubble, his skin as tight as a new-stretched drum. When he walked over to us, I sensed that he was still learning how to be—dare I say it—officious. His walk was transitional—that is, one could see the beginnings of the man in the orchestrations of the man-child. He wasn't yet fluid; somehow both stages equally claimed him—and thus he was, in a word, improvisational; and yet that he himself couldn't term it this way meant that he, unlike an artist, did not know how to use his inchoateness; that there was, that is, much mystery and little mastery.

If he was not an artist, my mother was, and she welcomed the opportunity like a raptor. The young registrar walked over, and my mother began her speech. "Young man, you don't know what it means to live a lie. You're young. But I'm near seventy, I won't be here much longer, and it's important to me and my family that I be who I am. The doctor listed me incorrectly as 'White' on my birth certificate, but I'm black. And proudly so. You, young man, there must be things you believe, things you would never betray?"

The young man looked sheepish, and I realized that this was taking all he'd learned at Harvard, or Boston University, or Holy Cross, and spinning it like a dervish. I watched the young boy's face search my mother's—he'd made a connection, and my mother saw it too.

"Young man, can you change the document, can you rectify a great wrong?"

The registrar began to say something about the document, but he stopped himself. Then, as if in a dream, he offered, "Oh, lady. Let me have your certificate." The young registrar briskly walked away, as if he had found his new legs, and disappeared behind a large screen. In about five minutes, he returned with a new birth certificate, with the race boldly listed as "Black," and presented it to my mother.

My mother was ecstatic; she wanted to kiss the boy. But she also perceived his newly assumed agency, and didn't wish to embarrass him. The registrar smiled broadly, evidencing his great pleasure. My mother and he had moved continents.

I don't know whether that young registrar changed my mother's color in the official state registry. I doubt if he did, although it is possible. For my mother, the truth had won out. For myself, it was another odd moment in a litany of racial episodes, all of which make sense, but only if you are an American and believe that an ounce of melanin, real or imagined, bespeaks something pivotal, foundational, and incontestable; only, that is, if you believe—like the doctor and my mother—in the American way, which, sadly, separates each of us from the other, in cemetery and housing project, love and industry, life and death. It means something to be black, my mother would proudly attest—and her life, indeed, proves as much, as does my life, and those that preceded it. And it means something to be white—which, too, is full of celebrations, disappointments, and incoherencies. And, at bottom, it means something to be American, which is the embodiment of all this deformation—the white and black, the black and white—this experiment which, many years ago, presented a white person and a black person with eyes that might have intuited anything but instead found solace in imagining how they differed, and created a legion of codes and prevarications so fantastic they approach the pathological.

Hungers:
Reflections on Affirmative Action

We could settle this whole race mess over a long lunch.
   —From a conversation overheard on a New York City bus

The pasts of his ancestors lean against
Him. Crowd him. Fog out his identity.
Hundreds of hungers mingle with his own,
Hundreds of voices advise so dexterously
He quite considers his reactions his,
Judges he walks most powerfully alone,
That everything is—simply what it is.
   —Gwendolyn Brooks, "The Sundays of Satin-Legs Smith"

Some months ago a good student of mine, during a luncheon to celebrate his fine stories, told me angrily that he had not been accepted to Harvard because of "affirmative action." Had this remark come from someone who was small-minded, racially insensitive, or less socially involved, I would have been saddened but not surprised. But that it came from a student who had worked in area prisons helping inmates to write better, who had struggled to increase his fraternity's awareness of social injustice, and who had, in wonderfully wrought stories, written tenderly about every manner of dispossession, I was sufficiently stymied. This student had written poignantly about a young woman's inability to see the implications of her own self-absorption, in prose as trenchant as Annie Dillard's; in a luminous novella, he deftly conveyed the small misfortunes of a romantic businessman, "lost in his own irrelevancies." Like Raymond Carver, with whom he shares much, my student's stories were always pithy, world-wise, and full of human empathy. He understood human beings, he was usually generous, and I expected much of him. But here, I was confronting someone hurt, sullen, and disconsolate—someone as cut off from good sense as a stone. It was painful and ugly.

As Gunnar Myrdal quipped, race in America seems to turn everybody insane. And this occurs, I think, because race, in this country, remains the province of the patently unexamined. Race—whatever else it is—is a notion informed by a multiplicity of tributary ones, all involving our difficult, ill-explored histories, and all inexorably personal. That we fail to understand America's racial past—as James Baldwin brilliantly shows—stems from a congress of self-deceptions and self-deformations, all of which, in various guises, seem to inhabit us like errant cells. On the one hand, we speak about our "great progress," and there has been much progress indeed, as I am the first to concede; on the other—and with far too great frequency—we seem to confront the inevitable paralysis: why won't the racial problem end? What do *these* people want? Why the incessant, dreary carping about race?

Much of this "racial fatigue" stems, I submit, from America's unique ability to view race as something we've largely confronted, since it has been with us for so long, and we've spent so much psychic time on it. (Here, of course, we confront the American penchant to confuse involvement with evolvement, as if spending a week with an unopened book is the same thing as reading it.) And by the same token, Americans are afraid to acknowledge how *painfully* personal our confrontation with race is, as if such a concession would dislodge the Earth's axis. And yet one has simply to look at our fiction, from Melville to Faulkner, Emerson to Cheever, to comprehend how indissolubly race remains at the center of the American psyche—it haunts us, like that terrible white whale, reminding us that it is our imaginings of "the other," indeed, which can send us to hell. And, of course, it is not simply our imaginings, but how we act on them, that is central: rape, lynching, Jim Crow, "separate but equal," three-fifths of a person, miscegenation laws, slavery. Whatever else can be said, our confrontation with race, certainly, has been dramatic, brutal, and agonizing. That we haven't been able to respond adequately to our participation in this mess, that we will argue that slaves are stupid and incapable of learning on the one hand and then punish them and their benefactors for teaching them to read on the other, this illogic, quite frankly, enters the realm of the pathological.

Much of the affirmative action debate is focused, at least in the media, on the ideal of fairness. Is it fair to use legal or academic remedies to reverse previous historical wrongdoings? Are the sins of the fathers and mothers vested on the children? Should my child be made to pay for the horrors of slavery, even if she had nothing to do with them? And on and on. But the real sting of affirmative action as it is experienced by whites, I maintain, is that it reaffirms—and my student certainly feels this, even if he hasn't fully understood its ramifications—that the world is often capricious, unintelligible, and brutal. My student *feels* it; but he does not yet understand its fullest implications, and these implications, I would argue, are essential to understanding the world and his place in it.

Let's look again at my student's situation. As I suggested, he had applied to Harvard, he had done very well in his classes, he had good SAT scores, and he is extremely talented. By his own lights, he deserved to get admitted. And yet he was not.

Now, let's look at Harvard's predicament. They, as Cornell, get thousands of applications for a very limited number of spots. Harvard's admissions officers will tell you that they could responsibly admit 90 percent of their applicants, although the actual admissions rate in 2002 was 11 percent. Thus, my student, as well as many others, could well have been admitted. And yet let's take this simple-minded conjecture further. If we exclude all of the people of color, less than 7 percent of the entering class, my student still has only the faintest hope of acceptance. Yes, those few minority students did foreclose some of his possibility to attend Harvard—and many of those minority students, interestingly, would have been admitted no matter what the criteria (Harvard gets the *best* students in the country). And, just as poignantly, legacies (students whose relatives attended Harvard) took up 25 percent of the places in the admitted class. Unless my student's father or mother attended Harvard/Radcliffe, he was even more numerically displaced by these students. And we should also include the bevy of talented athletes, and others who were admitted, say, for being violin virtuosos, who are also important to a university's sense of itself. In all honesty, there is a universe of variables here, and I haven't begun to discuss the fact that human beings, in a room, read those admissions folders—human beings who, variously impassioned, decide who would make the best Harvard student. It is all, frankly, a creative act of social engineering—it's a universe defined and shaped by people who, in W. D. Snodgrass's rhetoric, are "all vaguely furiously driven." This is not to say that the admissions board does not know what it is doing, or what it intends the Harvard class to look like; it is simply to state that the human imprecates everything.

My student at lunch, understandably, was not being analytical about his situation: he was hurt. And yet this brings me to a larger truth. He was hurt, and his hurt, at least from *his* vantage point, could be explained. It was those people of color who had denied him his Harvard placement, not the vagaries of an admissions process, where not everyone, sadly, can be admitted. Injustice is always easier to bear if it can be explained; and, understandably, it was far easier for my student to believe that black and Latino students (whatever their qualifications) were the cause of his disappointment than to interrogate the absurdities of an often-indifferent universe. And then, too, if affirmative action was at the heart of Harvard's decision, my student's performance was never truly in question, at least as he imagines it. That his good work was not as meritorious as another admitted Harvard student; that he was not as creative or as intellectually enterprising as John Winthrop from Temple, Nebraska, or Ken Smith from Harlem; that his lack of playing the piano, or the truth that he played the piano gracelessly—all of this, of course, was not important to my student's calculus. Undoubtedly, there were any number of reasons why my student was not accepted. Years ago, when I sent a poem to *The Nation* in the hope of getting my first acceptance in a national magazine, the editor penned me a quixotic note. "Dear Ken McClane," he wrote, "had this been Monday I would have accepted this." The editor was telling me, and it was important knowledge, that national magazines get hundreds of submissions—good, even interesting, poems often get turned down. Had my poems come earlier in the week, the editor might have been more accommodating, and I could swagger about, my poem soon to appear. But "time and chance" intervened, or, as my students are wont to say, "Shit happens." Sadly, we don't always get what we deserve or desire.

The weight of my student's pain is, of course, real—and I do not wish to diminish it. But his pain has nothing to do with affirmative action, and much to do, I hazard, with life's peccadilloes. We spend most of our lives trying to ensure our futures, to forestall suffering: parents want the best for their offspring; I want to create the best opportunities for myself. It is understandable, in a terrifying universe, to want to bring shape and contour to the incommensurate. But there are no givens in life. No one can ensure that she will take a breath tomorrow, or see the moon tonight. We can try—we can seek to mitigate the possible and diminish the ponderous—but the world, alas, does what it does.

Now, this is not an earthshaking revelation. And yet my student must realize that his anger was ill placed; that his pain, in reality, could only teach him something if he would unpack it; if he would, like the finest critic or watchmaker, interrogate its inner mechanisms, its springs, joinings, and dalliances. My student was suffering because it hurt to be denied—and yet one is often not listened to, taken into account, corroborated. As the spiritual laments, "Lord, why leave me here?"

To a large degree, my student's failure to comprehend his predicament stems from a lapse of imagination. He could not, or would not, interrogate the machinations of judgment—in the first instance, because it was painful; in the second, because, at bottom, it would suggest, alas, that there are intelligences (ways of seeing, valuable ones) he can barely fathom. For that black student from Harlem, who was accepted at Harvard, may have been smarter than my student: he may have had higher board scores, class rank, and intellectual heft; or he, just as importantly, might have been the first student in his ghetto school to take advanced calculus, daily venturing to Columbia University, after he took care of his aged grandmother and five siblings, and before he worked five hours a night at the local pharmacy. This narrative, of course, my student would fail to contemplate, since his own sojourn, one culled out of hurt and disappointment, caused him to be imaginatively lead-footed. The gift of the imagination, ultimately, is the gift to appreciate another: to see, alas, that I am in you and you are in me.

And this is why the affirmative action debate has so befuddled so many potentially well-meaning people. The argument which suggests that we need a "race-neutral society," though offered with good intentions by some, is a spurious one—it conveys, at least to people of color, that their historical experience is either a hindrance to community, or is of no importance, which, of course, is hardly palatable to someone who loves her "colored" self, and finds in her color, as she should, much to be proud. And this reasoning suggests, once again, a terrible paucity of imagination: whites, for their part, have often had the privilege of acting as if they were "color blind," although their legalisms, in court and country club, suggest quite the opposite. And, until recently, whites have not had to see their color as a badge of privilege, power, or malfeasance; they have not been made to see themselves as white.

And yet people of color have always viewed their pigmentation as an essential barometer of their historical reality— of who and what they are—albeit in far different ways than often envisioned by their countrymen. As Gwendolyn Brooks and Toni Morrison evince, a people's struggle to survive is never merely a litany of dispossession, pain, or nullification: no one is a mere sociological construct. No matter how deformative slavery was, blacks forged lives, created art, and made their exalted way in the world. If I am the benefactor of the Collegiate School, the oldest private school in America, I am also the offspring of 147th Street in Harlem, where I learned to celebrate the quiet decency of those around me: those who had been given so little materially and yet proffered so much spiritually. To deny race, at bottom, is to deny them.

After a long discussion, my student, to his credit, began the process of examining his anger. He let go of his cloying to half-truths; he sensed, and powerfully, what it meant to enter the deep water, where failure cannot be explained or reasoned away. This, I think, is the hardest thing for a human being to accept: that life cannot always be tamed, or channeled; that life, at bottom, is terrifying. My student, in the weeks to come, began to listen more to those inmates he tutored; he began to take their stories to heart, to see in their private invocations their desire to see the world made anew. "I never really listened to them before," he told me. "I never understood how much I could learn from them. I never realized that we're all so frightened and vulnerable. I never realized," he said very slowly, "that they held the key for me."

I was very proud of my student.

Musicals

Don't let it be forgot
That there once was a spot
For one brief, shining moment
Called Camelot.

—Camelot, *lyrics by Alan Jay Lerner*

But it was only love which could accomplish the miracle
of making a life bearable—only love, and love itself
mostly failed.

—*James Baldwin,* Another Country

Although I do have a trace of the romantic about me,
which, of course, is the poet's stock-in-trade, I try not to suc-
cumb to the obvious attractions of sheer otherworldliness—
that is, though I understand the obvious allure of believing in
the shamanistic or the inherent integration of all things, I'm

not easily a passenger on the new wave express, or at least I like to assert that I am not. Part of this reservation stems, I guess, from my personality: I'm usually cautious, and I like to keep my enthusiasms close to my chest. And part of this, too, celebrates the fact that I am attracted to those who are realists—to those who make decisions, fight in the rough-and-tumble, to those, that is, who *act*. My father was one of these people, and I will recall an incident that brilliantly encapsulates why he was so wondrous to me, and how he showed me—in word *and* action—why I am a bundle of two hopefully reconcilable strivings.

When I was eight, after I had asked my father, for the umpteenth time, what he did for work, he took me to the hospital. After verbally trying to convey what a doctor does, and seeing that I was not getting it, he consented, with some trepidation, to *show* me, as a kind of practicum. That day, we both had to wear white scrubs, and mine was so long they had to cinch it with adhesive, a pretty nurse telling me, probably ill-advisedly, that I looked so professional that I might get confused for the surgeon. This suggestion, of course, terrified me, since all I could imagine was my untutored hands in someone's guts.

As I recall, the operating room was sparkling, with new-fangled instruments, all inviting a tangle of wires that seemed to disappear into a giant cylinder; near the wall, aslant from the blackened window, were machines that held bulbous globes, hosting what looked like cotton suspended in the air, pelting against the glass enclosure, like addled birds. Nurses were running to and fro; technicians—working dials—were intently listening to my father's every syllable; here everything seemed to depend on him, as if he were the hospital's Leonard Bernstein. For the first time in my life, I was not the center of his attention, and I felt unnecessary.

After far too long, my father gently took my arm and ushered me into a side room, leaving all the busy people. He explained that he had to hack through a massive bit of bone to repair an artery, "Ken," my father said. "First, I want to make certain that you wish to see this—it may be ugly, and there will be some blood." And then he said something I'll never forget. "Ken, your mother is an artist, and I love her for that. She paints and writes; she sees things in a way I never can, but always want to. But this is what *I* do. I have to make a choice, I have to commit myself, and I can't have any second thoughts. Do you understand me? I'm different from your mother. And you are both of us."

And then my father began the operation, cutting the bone with a short, hard-edged saw. The bone did not separate easily. I saw my father sweat; I saw him tug and yaw and attack. For some reason, I had thought that the operation would be less physical, that the bone would sever quickly, and that my father would swiftly be on to the next step, the intricate arterial mapping, the *skilled* work. But this part was *willful:* my father could have no qualms: he simply had to cut.

So, mindful of my father's life, and his generous parable, I feel great anguish at suggesting that I tend towards the dreamy, although I am also my mother's child, as he so well celebrated. Still, I grew up on musicals in the 1950s and 1960s, and they were my first real association with art as provender for hope and possibility. In my house, we didn't go to movies, we went to the theatre. And the theatre was serious business. In fact, my parents never attended the cinema. Oh, to be truthful, there was one grand exception, when my brother and I were extras in the movie *Jaws,* but that shouldn't count. It was filmed on Martha's Vineyard, where my parents owned a house, and they attended the *Jaws* opening, which they supremely tolerated; yet they never viewed the movie again, even though they were unabashedly doting parents. "The movies are phony," my father used to say, and that was that.

And just as truthfully, I've existed in America largely by imagining an America in which I could live—which is, I would argue, the lot of most black people. The America I confronted—in the streets of Harlem and the diminishments of my private school—*needed* my improvements if I were to survive it, and I am not overstating this. America, at least for me, was a difficult proposition, and not for the usual reasons. I could not claim, as had Richard Wright, that Jim Crow had brutally scarred me: I hadn't seen a lynching up close, or smelled the burning flesh in my nostrils; I hadn't been driven to leave America, or to write *Native Son*. Yet I had suffered. At my school, I was routinely singled out and punished, sometimes because of my race; but just as often, I hazard, because of the person I was, although the person I was and the race that accompanied it seemed difficult to disentangle.

At bottom, it was bewildering to leave my Harlem home and venture down to the Collegiate School, the oldest private school in America, founded in 1626. Since I was one of the first two blacks in the school's 300-year history—arriving in 1957 in the first grade—I was largely an experiment: the school had no idea about my two professional parents, me, or the student I might become. And I was just as clueless about the school's aims. In my first week of classes, I was welcomed into the school; in the second week, John Ewing called me a "nigger" and I punched him in the mouth; by week three, I was in the headmaster's office facing suspension.

I must relate that when I hit John Ewing, I was doing my parents' bidding. Whatever else I had been told—and remember that my father was a physician, my mother, a licensed pharmacist and writer—there were two cardinal rules in my family. At no time was I to permit anyone to call me stupid or to deride my race. As my mother told me, if someone calls you either, "Hit him, please." And in retrospect this injunction, though fraught with implications, especially for a somewhat retiring child, served me well. Although I was to be put to the test a few times, I would always measure up. And that nagging sense of inferiority, that spine-damaging, ruinous imprecation that you must accept what someone terms you, no matter how belittling it might be, could never take hold. My parents understood that the world would find innumerable ways to cast you low—it was essential that you not abet it. *Niggers did not fight back*, was the implication here, and if you think of Frederick Douglass's *Narrative*, my parents had it right. The slavemaster tended to beat the docile slave, not the self-possessed one; the slavemaster, to no one's surprise, was hardly courageous. So that little defiance—which, I must add, was so out of keeping with everything else in my background (we didn't curse, we didn't steal, and we didn't, with this one exception, fight)—became axiomatic.

A diet of musicals, I now realize, permitted me the wherewithal to conjure up a reality largely of my own making, one that at least employed a different coda. If *Camelot* or *Brigadoon* did nothing else, they affirmed that there was an alternative reality—that what you saw in the streets of Harlem, or in the repressive walls of the Collegiate School, was not everything. It's not a new idea to suggest that art permits one voyages, or to argue that art can make a dreary life less so. But for me, those musicals were the greatest illustration that another world existed: one that held music, joy, and unfettered access to the extraordinary.

In truth, again and again, the theatre seemed forever to impress itself on my family, as if it were our Plymouth Rock. I recall hearing about José Ferrer and Paul Robeson's visit to our house during the opening run of *Othello* on Broadway, when my family lived with Congressman Adam Clayton Powell, in his large apartment building on 147th Street. Robeson, of course, was brilliant, magnificent in stature and voice, and controversial (especially for his pro-socialist leanings), and *Othello*, understandably in mid-1940s racialized America, held everyone's attention. As my parents recounted it, during the first week onstage, an overwrought white patron literally yelled, "Stop!" when Robeson, as Othello, placed his great hands around Desdemona's "fair" neck. José Ferrer laughed when he detailed how Robeson initially loosened his grip upon hearing the man. This was 1940s America: black people were being lynched routinely; he, the great Robeson, was not immune. "Kill her," Ferrer remonstrated, under his breath, and Robeson returned to the play, finally honoring Shakespeare's intentions.

There were two musicals that my family attended again and again, Richard Rodgers and Oscar Hammerstein's *South Pacific* and Alan Jay Lerner and Frederick Loewe's *Camelot*. *South Pacific,* as you recall—along with a good bit of racist tripe (the fawning Bloody Mary character, for example)— recounts the love between a Frenchman and a young American nurse on a South Sea Island during World War II; and it also, to a lesser degree, proffers the narrative of a young lieutenant and his love for a Polynesian woman. There's a great deal of the usual romantic anxiety in the plot: will the sophisticated Frenchman win the innocent young nurse? But, most important, and certainly for my parents, *South Pacific,* albeit cumbersomely, confronted the implications of race, at a time when so few mainstream vehicles dared.

For my parents, the young lieutenant's story was the riveting one. As warriors have since time immemorial, the lieutenant falls in love with the young Pacific Islander, and his world is turned upside down. How can he love someone so different, who is also yellow? Will the lieutenant be able to put aside his ill-digested American prejudice and follow his heart? I recall how my parents would hold hands during the musical, singing with the actors, their eyes afire with the hard-fought idealism of love conquering all. They understood— and all too poignantly—when Lieutenant Cable sang: *You've got to be taught to hate and fear. . . . You've got to be taught to be afraid . . . Of people whose eyes are oddly made . . . And people whose skin is a different shade.*

I should relate that my father and mother had difficult sojourns navigating this great Republic. My father was the first black doctor in twenty-five years to graduate from a

Boston medical school, a bitter process that I have described elsewhere, and he graduated third in his class. During his training, when my father was set to examine white patients, they often asked him to locate another doctor, one "who knew something." A number of white patients simply refused to be touched by him.

In later years, my father would have trouble finding a medical residency, buying a house in Cape Cod, and enjoying the "perks" blithely shown his fellow doctors. At Columbia Presbyterian Hospital in New York City—where my father taught fourth-year medical students for forty years—he never received private patient privileges, which meant that his patients had to be under the supervision of another doctor while they remained in the hospital. My father could make the admitting diagnosis, but he could never ensure that his patients would find a bed, nor could he guarantee that he would be their personal physician, and this, of course, was enormously humiliating to my father *and* his patients. Although my father was one of the best internists on the staff— and was responsible for diagnosing one of the most complex strains of hyperthyroidism in the medical literature—he was treated as a mere neophyte. As Dr. David Spain, one the world's preeminent forensic pathologists, told me: "Your father was the finest clinician on the entire staff. Had he been born a generation later, or had the medical school administration been less prejudiced, he would have been head of the department."

My mother suffered, too, albeit differently. A graduate of Girls Latin School in Boston, one of the premier public schools in the nation, she was even more brilliant than was my father. After she graduated from Massachusetts College of Pharmacy as Salutatorian of her class, she couldn't find a job in New York City, no matter how hard she tried. In her case, it was not racial; it involved her gender. She would apply for jobs as a pharmacist, and little would come of it. After six months of looking, she accepted the obvious: she had better change her career. Sadly, she never practiced pharmacy. In a few weeks, she mastered the stock market and worked on Wall Street; then she moved on to writing and editing; and then, in her final years, she began to paint, working diligently at the famous Arts Students League.

For my parents, *South Pacific* explored what the first slave pondered when she was brought to these shores: Would this brutal country ever be able to celebrate her possibilities? Would we, like that young Pacific Islander, be brought into the fold? Lieutenant Cable's song, "Younger Than Springtime," with its hopefulness and promises for rebirth, was more than a lovely ditty for my parents—it was America's myth incantatory. That the lieutenant would later die seemed inevitable; interracial love in America is a dangerous notion: it can kill you. And certainly, to be fair, it permitted Rodgers and Hammerstein the province to intimate a world that could be different, a world where hate could be conquered and sent packing. Sadly, of course, the lieutenant never received the opportunity to test his new liberalism—one wonders if love, at least in those turbulent times, could withstand America; and clearly Rodgers and Hammerstein, realists that they were, were not willing to find out.

Camelot, too, is a great love story. Unlike *South Pacific, Camelot*—though rich with intrigue, carnival, and verbal and musical élan—is far more tragic. Although Lancelot and Guinevere do find each other, and their love is cause for some of the finest balladry in recent musical history, King Arthur's kingdom is brutally destroyed. Arthur's final lament on the field of battle—after he sees Lancelot and Guinevere, his friend and wife, now allied against him in love and war— seemed wonderfully to complement what African Americans were feeling: we had paid a terrible price to honor the American myth, and yet it, at every turn, was betraying us. That this musical appeared in the 1960s is not surprising: the world was indeed burning—with the war in Vietnam and the civil rights struggle—and my parents, like all black people in the U.S., were mired in that complex swampland where the country would either perish in fire and hate or find some new provident compromise. Now, sadly, one could not simply murder the lieutenant as in *South Pacific:* we'd passed beyond that quaint literary two-step.

At the end of *Camelot,* my parents were always tear-filled. These tears evidenced how much they appreciated Arthur's divided loyalties: Arthur, at least in the musical, loved Lancelot and Guinevere. He would have liked to step aside, even gracefully, and let the lovers go, sparing his kingdom and the known world. But the time and the world would not have it: the world invariably wanted blood; it was comfortable with the feudal.

This hard-smacking, tough reminder held my parents at *Camelot*'s end, for they had to confront the grueling human calculus that has bedeviled slave and poet alike for generations: are we capable of that world we imagine, one in which each of us is sacred? My parents' hands, often at this moment, would find mine—and act powerfully out of keeping with their strict New England upbringing, where one did not touch, as if such a minute exchange might set the planets awash. This gesture, in fact, celebrated the last time my family was *truly* a family: When my brother was dying of alcoholism in New York, spending what would be his last few days in Roosevelt Hospital, I took my parents to see *Camelot* at City Center, as a way to take our mind off my brother who was lying comatose, twenty blocks away. If it seemed odd to leave my brother at that juncture, you do not know what it is to confront a loved one dying, nor do you realize how important a balm the theatre was for us. There was little to be done for my brother: we needed, I guess, more precisely, to reimagine ourselves.

At Arthur's behest to the young lad that he keep alive the myth of Camelot and run away from the conflagration, our hands would touch momentarily. We'd envision the world aflame, the war raging, the Kingdom imperiled: this was a world we knew all too intimately. Then, just as powerfully, we'd remember that young lad, still alive, who held—like the grandest secret—the chalice of hope: *things could get better; they, certainly, might get worse too; but they could get better.* And then we would begin the fast journey back into ourselves, savoring that tiny moment, that small consolation, before the world, this day or the next, would inform us, in such a brutal American way, what despicable vessels we all are.

A Love Note:
A. R. Ammons as Teacher

and because whatever is
moves in weeds
and stars and spider webs
and known
        is loved:
in that love,
each of us knowing it,
I love you.
        —A. R. Ammons, *"Identity"*

I first met A. R. Ammons at the behest of a woman I was dating when I was a freshman at Cornell in 1969. As a black student from Harlem who missed the City, I had begun to write what I then considered to be poems. To be brutally honest, I didn't know anything about poetry: to me good intentions and a fistful of pain were art; my suffering was enough. That my creations were largely eruptions of my own distress was something I had yet to learn, and most powerfully. Add to that dreary mix the Vietnam War, the deaths of Dr. Martin Luther King and Malcolm X, my lust-ridden body and my proverbial loneliness, and you now have my mental state. My girlfriend, who understood much more about art and its rigors than I, wanted me to meet "the famous American poet" who taught at the university. I didn't know who A. R. Ammons was, and the fact that he was a great American writer meant little to me. I simply wanted to be corroborated.

In those days, Mr. Ammons's office was located on the second floor of Lincoln Hall and he was directing the Center for the Creative and the Performing Arts, the last time I believe he ever undertook administration. Later on, Ammons would move to the second floor of Goldwin Smith Hall, where E. B. White, Vladimir Nabokov, and Carl Becker had maintained offices, but that day he was still in Lincoln, sitting behind his unusually large desk, topped with an abundance of scraggly plants and a large ficus angling towards the light, like some paean to survival. Archie tended to love plants that were pot-bound and floundering: he coveted—I think in most things—those things most bedraggled and tossed out.

I can vividly recall handing Mr. Ammons a sheaf of poems, which he gracefully accepted, and his offer to read my poems in a week's time. As a teacher of creative writing, I now understand what a great imposition such requests are; and I know that Ammons—then, as always—was besieged with the irrepressible output of a legion of young who felt that they had something essential to say. That day, Ammons ended our meeting by saying in a very slow southern drawl, "I'll see you next week."

I did not return. In truth, I felt there was nothing he, a white man, from North Carolina, could tell me. At the time I didn't know anything about Southerners, and I painted them all with a broad stroke, something of which I am not very proud. To me, Archie was a symbol of that litany of racial violence—beginning in 1619 and moving to Selma—a legacy that had hurt me, in many profound and ill-understood ways. I didn't know much—I was a head full of the transgressive and the transgressed—and I was angry. That Archie would become my greatest champion was something I had yet to learn; that we would spend hours talking, become friends and later colleagues, forging an alliance that was as strong as it was sometimes difficult, this, too, was all in the future.

Little did I know then that Archie and I were beginning that difficult dance which taints all relationships between writers: we had work to do, we had to be self-invested, and the thing which made us care for one another, the art, was as ravenous as a Minotaur.

Later, at times, we would have arguments about what a poem could achieve. Here I would argue for writing needing to be political—what else could I believe?—and he, of course, would challenge the narrowness of my beliefs. In truth, I knew he was right; in truth, I suspect, Archie knew I could argue little else. Sadly, at these moments, we were all too human and all too different: our connection made difficult, I submit, because it was a connection.

But in 1970, as luck would have it, I would sign up for Creative Writing, and lo and behold, the teacher was A. R. Ammons. Mr. Ammons never mentioned our previous meeting; he might not have remembered it, although I doubt if that was the case. He, most probably, had the forbearance to excuse my previous lapse, while I, for my part, remained silent. Let me simply state that the class was a wonderful one, and I am glad to this day that fate brought me beyond my own prejudice.

Ammons ran the seminar in a gentle, nonhierarchical way. He did not assign exercises or demand that students experiment, say, with the villanelle or the sonnet form. What Ammons desired was for students to write as their imaginations dictated. It was the writing (and the need to write) that would offer the impetus for refining and divining craft: it was the writing that would suggest one's own individuality. Here, of course, Archie was listening to his own experience. He had not been taught to write in a writing program; he, in truth, had little respect for them. His poems came from his need to convey his wonderment, to find meaning "in the moon-tossed and the vanquished," to invoke those things "left out."

Ammons's method was uniquely suited to me and to many others. What he affirmed was that, for him, you were sacred, in all your dilapidation. And for the multitude of us who were the intellectually unwashed, this was the greatest confirmation. Ammons permitted us to speak from a position of strength; we were not simply the raging, the uncouth, the crazed; we were not, that is, what our parents feared. No, we had something precious to relate if only we could honor it. And our own entanglements, our awkwardness, our incoherence, could create heady music.

Ammons's classes were wonderful for another reason. Although we didn't spend a great deal of time talking about famous poets—we rarely read other poets, we never read Archie's poems—we did sense that poetry was the highest calling. Much of this came from the workshop setting itself— we were convened as a congress of wisdoms, impertinences, and enthusiasms; much of this came, no doubt, from the undeniable brilliance of Ammons himself. When he spoke about poems, one felt as if one were in the presence of this century's Coleridge or Dr. Johnson. And indeed one was.

Crucially, Ammons's sense of the world was so omnipresent that when one listened to him, one was, in truth, walking in one of his poems. Quintessentially, when Archie was serious (and not playing around or doing his "I'm just a country boy"/hick routine), one could simply put line breaks in his elegant oratory, and it would be an Ammons poem. Disconcertingly, for those of us who wanted to be practitioners, it was as if his poems came from some marvelous, bottomless fount. Archie, seemingly, had only to open his mouth and revelation flowed. This, of course, was not always true. But Archie did appear like a poetic medium, a channeler of the consequential. Writing may have been difficult for him, I know at times it was, but still when it came—and it always came—it spewed torrential and provident. To my knowledge, I can think of only one other contemporary poet so closely attuned, in speech and life, to her verse, Gwendolyn Brooks, who, incidentally, we lost just a few months before Ammons.

Yet the greatest aspect of Archie as mentor was his absolute belief in human individuality and the poem as the ultimate embodiment of truth. As he instructed me in an unpublished poem, "Improvisations for the Main Man Ken McClane":

> Since poetry declares nothing ever
> even in its fantasies and lies
> but the truth
> I do not
> guide the declarations shallow,
> canalized, into only what
> I would hear or have heard:
> If the truth is
> as it is
> unavoidable
> it need not be pursued
> and cannot be fled:
> But there, profound,
> dissolved,
> it doesn't prick your feet with
> thorns
> but sustains you merely into your

own endeavor:
truth that deep is perhaps
no longer truth.

For many of us who have learned from him, it was
Archie's irrepressible restlessness that so made us love him.
Archie would not lie, he understood the demolitions in the
depths, the danger of a wisdom too highly prized, and he
asked that we be willing to risk presence, that we not heed the
merely easy, the fatuous, or the pretty. In class, his comments
on poems tended to be more general than local. Although he
was interested in a word or line—his rich "That's nice" often
declaring his joy—Archie tended to engage in large claims
and "constellations" of meaning. His method seemed more
an affirmation of our small announcements than the nuts
and bolts of the poem as thing. Whenever someone would
claim that a poem should do this—say, no poem should be a
political tract, or no one should write a "love poem"—Archie,
deftly, would find a million ways to prove that poet's criticism
ill considered. There are no boundaries on love or poetry,
he would say. As he was wont to remind us, "critics are untan-
glers, poets tangle": our work as poets "is to work wonders."

Once a colleague in the English Department came up to
him and asked him in a group of poets if he had read a new
book on Wallace Stevens. Archie looked at this self-satisfied
critic who, I guess, thought he was making good conversation, and said, with a twinkle in his eye, but not without a
touch of anger, "We do not get paid to read books. We get
paid to write them. You read us." Those of us who were writers welcomed that tongue-lashing. In the academy, all too
often, we are the whipping boys of the scholars who somehow forget that they write about us—that a dead writer was
once living. Archie would not brook this. He knew how fragile we all were; he knew, and intimately, how much one could
suffer.

It was wonderful to be taught by an elder who saw us as knowledgeable, sacred, in-process, and gifted. I remember how he would prize something I said or wrote because it was out of the academy, street-wise, extraordinary, or simply true. That we at times didn't appreciate all that he committed to us is understandable; that he remained a tireless defender of our rights to our authority—to our "Truths"—shall remain with me as the greatest instruction.

The 13th Juror

Life rarely confirms one's preoccupations, but last summer, after three successful evasions of jury duty, I finally had to produce myself for jury selection. It was not in New York City—where everything teems with intrigue and humanity—but in a small town in upstate New York, with a college and a well-known university, where if people do not always know one another, they do know someone, down the hill or at the shopping mall, who can attest to their child's shoe size. The town is, in the old adage, a good place to raise one's kids and oneself. And yet it has its problems: the schools are good, but poor children do not do as well as those with wealth. And there is much discussion—by supposed people of goodwilll—about the value of tracking, with the successful, by and large, supporting their privilege, while the others—spurned and voiceless—grow increasingly disaffiliated and sullen. Still, Ithaca is a good town for America, and I do not mean this facetiously.

I have witnessed the justice system in other less tranquil places: I grew up in Harlem; and, as my wife reminds me, I am the only black male she knows who has not been falsely arrested (or at least placed under suspicion) by the police. I really do not know why I have been so lucky; my brother certainly saw more than his fill of the justice system. Indeed, at age six, Paul had his first run-in with a cop: someone had her wallet stolen; my brother was convenient; he was also young and black. However cogent his small protestations, Paul was subsequently detained at the police station until my father arrived. Can you imagine being in police custody, at age six? From that moment on, my brother never liked the police. Indeed, I recall how he would always say, his contempt seemingly bottomless, "See the City's finest. They *love* to help you." And then his body would tighten, the rage seeming to harken from a depth prehistoric. "I'd kill those white motherfuckers if I could," he would say. Paul would later die of alcoholism, in a tale too dreary to recount here, but I can't help thinking that his fate, however embrionically, was sealed in that first police encounter.

In Ithaca, where I live and teach, such things rarely happen. It is a university town, and for that reason the police are disposed to treat the citizens with respect: the police know for what they are paid and by whom. The police in New York City realize the same thing: they are paid to keep order, which means, if you live in Harlem, the South Bronx, or Bedford-Styvesant, then you are always suspect. But in Ithaca, New York, the police and the court well understand the community in which they reside. If you are called for jury duty and are a college teacher, they appreciate that a professor cannot easily miss weeks of classes: students pay to learn about literature from a specialist; a university—no matter how rich it is—does not have spare scholars available for any calamity. And so, in Ithaca at least, the faculty are routinely excused from jury duty during the academic term, from September to June; and I, through luck and bureaucratic caprice, had evaded "the call" for three years.

I, unlike many, did not mind the obligation to serve as a juror. I welcomed it. As someone who had always been interested in human psychology and our fragile human attempts at community, participating in the justice system possessed obvious attractions. I would see how people came to be judged in a small town; I would witness the complex—albeit often difficult—deliberations of human beings as they tried to understand the actions of another; and I would have the opportunity to see if I, as a participant, could act judiciously.

A trial in a small town—despite the general degradation of American institutions—is a miraculous paean to democracy, one that would make the Founding Fathers proud. The jury I was to serve upon was asked to adjudicate a case involving a young woman accused of driving while intoxicated. The woman had recently been divorced, and she had other attendant problems—including a dislike for authority, which her lawyer attempted to manipulate—but she had not, as is so often the case, hurt anyone in a horrible accident. She simply had imbibed too much; and, in a bad turn of luck, had passed too near to a New York State Trooper, who, that afternoon, had been ticketing another driver for speeding, his patrol car parked at the highway's edge. After the woman's car came dangerously close to the officer's foot—almost "creasing his pants," as the stoic trooper described it—he followed her for a few miles, watching her weave here and there, and then pulled her over. Initially, the woman was cooperative with the officer. However, after a few questions, she became angry. Finally, he asked her to take a "field sobriety test"—five exercises that ascertain one's mental and physical dexterity. The woman passed the first three, relatively easily; she failed the latter two. After the patrolman had reason to believe that the woman was legally drunk—any failure of the sobriety test substantiates such a finding—she was asked to remain in his police car while he examined her vehicle. And here began an extraordinary sequence, reminiscent of a Laurel and Hardy comedy skit, as the woman repeatedly attempted to vacate the officer's car. Although she was "loosely belted in," three times she extricated herself from the trooper's car and ran across the tarmac, and each time she was retrieved and asked again to remain sitting in the passenger seat. On the fourth attempt, however, the woman, amazingly, grabbed the policeman's radio mike and cried to the dispatcher, "Someone is imprisoning me." It was, as you can well imagine, a wild scene.

In Ithaca, as I presume elsewhere, preliminary jury selection is conducted by the judge, who asks the potential jurors—in groups of twelve at a time—a number of general questions involving the juror's past and his or her ability to be impartial. The day I was called, there was a jury pool of some eighty Ithacans, of various ages, professions, and nationalities. Some people I knew from Cornell; most, of course, I did not. A few people clearly did not want to serve: their answers were riffled with indecision or a cusp of bitterness; a few others, for religious reasons, asked to be excused.

Once the group was substantially thinned, the judge asked each of us to convey any information about our lives we felt might be important to the court. Incredibly, in the first group of twelve, each person recounted a tragedy of oceanic proportions: one man had recently lost his son to drugs; another woman's husband had been diagnosed with AIDS; another, a young man who spoke in a whisper—with a shock of unruly red hair—had just learned that he, in a few weeks, would lose his hearing. It was sobering. At the time I had been consumed with my own worries about my mother's

headlong descent into Alzheimer's disease, and the death of
my alcoholic brother. I thought my trouble was unusual: I
wanted to think so. But on and on life's troubles flowed, and
how ill prepared we are for its scourges.

As luck would have it, after three hours, there were only
three people left in the courtroom, and the jury now had
eleven members. The judge asked the prosecuting attorney
for his two final names, and the defense for his. I listened
as one name was called—not really saddened that it wasn't
mine—and readied myself to go home. I had done my duty;
the jury was selected. But then, as I began to leave the room,
I heard the judge announce, "Kenneth A. McClane, you will
be the alternate. Please sit with the jury."

Being "the alternate juror" is a strange responsibility.
Your job is to act as a standby, should one of the real jurors
get sick. So I would hear the testimony, sit among the jury,
and yet would not be allowed to deliberate or to vote unless
someone fell ill. Somehow, this position seemed only fitting: it had been my life's lot—the watcher, the onlooker. As
a black person at an all-white prep school, I had been an
onlooker; as a child of two professionals in Harlem, I had
been an onlooker; in the English Department, at least for my
early years as one of its only two blacks, I had been an onlooker. So here I was again. Yet here, there was a twist: I could
witness all the events, but I could not, even if I wanted to,
become an *active* participant. In my past, I could—often with
great difficulty, at time to no effect—take a position, however
parochial. But here I was to be and not to be.

The trial, in truth, only lasted one day. The poor woman
was found guilty—and everybody wondered why she had even
brought the case to court. It would have seemed more pro-
pitious to entertain a plea bargain, since her actions in the
police car—the intemperate yelling over the police radio—
testified to someone clearly under the influence of more than
nerves. The others on the jury—the *real* jurors—couldn't

fathom a reason for her actions. But I, calling on that reservoir of fantasy and insight, culled after years of watching *and* doing, offered that she probably had a job where she could ill afford to receive a conviction for drunkenness—a position with the military, perhaps, or a big bank. It was all conjecture, of course. But before I could continue, one of the jurors reminded me—with not a small taint of disapproval—that it was exactly such "big thinking" that kept academics off most juries. And he, his red suspenders included, was largely correct.

At the time I did not have the proper rejoinder, but mulling over his statement, it again became clear to me why I relished being an outsider, or, at least, why I found myself condemned to such a position. The red-suspenders juror was indeed right. We cared little for the reason underlying the woman's actions: it didn't matter, it was immaterial, she was guilty. But it *did* matter that my brother was falsely accused, like thousands of other blacks, in a place seemingly a million miles from tranquil Ithaca. It matters because my brother *mattered,* because life is complex, because he died largely because he believed he didn't amount to much. It matters because love matters, and love demands that I invest myself in that woman, even if I can never truly understand her motivations, because I must understand my own self, which, though one may try to deny it, rests fundamentally on an appreciation of others. It matters, because all the pain in the world is *our* pain: deny it, if you will, but it comes back to haunt us in the ghetto, in the murder on the college campus, in the violence between husbands and wives, in our wars and our increasing transgressions. Deny it, and we continue to live as mere husks—the pain increasing, the answers less and less provident. Deny it, and the heart sours, love darkens, death looms everywhere, and we perish, lost to ourselves and the healing hope of others. Deny it—and you neglect the world's inescapable dictum: *in the eyes of one's victim one sees oneself.*

Driving

I have put off writing this for some time, largely because it was too painful for me to write about my parents, and largely too because I was worried that my experience—which is purely that, *my* experience—might cause others undue consternation. In all honesty, the first reason is the most telling: Alzheimer's disease is a horrendous aliment—it takes someone away, before the body is gone, and it diminishes that person in very small but codifiable ways. First, the loved one loses some of her vocabulary or seems stuck in the interstices of life, as if the film of one's daily happenings were cut, and one was living in a few frames, with the rest of the narrative unfolding in the next theater, which, somehow, one can readily see. For a powerful second, the two theatres are showing the same frame, but then things devolve, the correspondences unhinge, and both theatres grow shadowy—the film is still playing, there's even a show of delight on the loved one's face, but it is a private, peculiar delight, as hard to imagine as the joy of a snake cut in halves, its two severed pieces struggling for a rapprochement.

The disease, most centrally, is about loss and love, both so tightly entwined that I am reminded of a wonderful Chinese painting of a brilliant long-stemmed lily that I confronted a few years ago at the Johnson Art Museum at Cornell. Initially, the overwhelming flower seemed merely vibrant, resplendent, and triumphant. Its color was vital; its presence, incontestable. But then if one was attentive, one noticed a slight sliver of decay, like a small finger, at the bottom of the stem— one realized, that is, that beauty and destruction share the same root, that one undergirds the other. Alzheimer's sadly, God knows, presents the decimation and even, at times, the possibility of a flower; but there is no balance, no artifice. There is no suitable metaphor.

Still, this is a far too romantic vision of Alzheimer's, though it does convey some of my experience, even as it suggests how I was able to cope with it, putting to good use my literary skills. My father and mother both died of Alzheimer's, and both of them, in different ways, confronted the disease. My mother succumbed first. Indeed, my mother was a *perfect* Alzheimer's patient, if one can say that, since she presented all the neurological signs of the illness. At the time of my mother's diagnosis in the 1980s, the disease could only be confirmed by an autopsy, which, of course, was of little help. There were, however, six warning signs—if the patient obsessively turned her thumbs in a counterclockwise motion was one indicator; if the patient splayed her feet outward, as if she were chronically pigeon-toed, was another. As we used to joke, of the six indices, my mother exhibited seven. And please understand how important macabre humor became for my family, and for others with the illness, too—before the disease we used to laugh a great deal: it was lifeblood to us; after the disease, we laughed less, but we still found moments of utter hilarity. When your father, who was usually a bit tight with money, suddenly throws all of his twenties out the window—which happened to a friend of mine—what else are you to do?

If this seems rather clinical, I am writing this after ten years. When my mother first entered the nursing home, after we had exhausted every in-home possibility, she was her usual elegant self. My mother was quite beautiful—she had lovely hair, an olive complexion, and was quite svelte for someone in her eighties. In her earlier years she had a 50s movie star figure—"full-figured" was the term then, I believe. In those days, my mother loved donuts and pies; she always had a sweet tooth, and I recall how she would always pester me to get her a jelly donut, especially if it came right out of the baker's oven. Her new slim weight was largely a response to the disease, and one could see her ribs, poking out like small tubers. She wouldn't eat, or she would forget to eat; and when she was told to eat, since she needed the caloric content, she couldn't understand the concept.

Interestingly, in temperament, my mother remained largely the person she had been throughout the disease's ravages. When someone would come to visit, she would immediately tell her how beautiful she looked and how happy she was that she had come to see her. This was her characteristic gentility—she had been born in Boston, she had attended the famous Boston Girl's Latin School, and she was, in truth, a Black Boston aristocrat. Where she evidenced a profound departure from her strict Yankee upbringing was in her love for outlandish clothes and color, which corresponded, ultimately, to her not small success as a painter. My mother would wear wild green pants and always wanted her husband and children to jazz up their sedate clothing palette—something that my father often did, God knows, to alarming affect. In her artwork, there was always a rhapsody of invention, involving boisterous, even hysterical colors that would have astonished Hieronymus Bosch. If she was reserved in manner, her inner soul was irrepressible.

With her wonderful manners, my mother also evolved incredible coping skills. As she realized that her faculties were diminishing, she employed a brilliant ruse to keep up pretenses. When I came to visit her one day, I asked her, rather self-servingly, if she knew what my name was. Now, this is a question that almost all Alzheimer's family members employ as an essential calculus: if the loved one remembers your name, she is still present; she still shares a reality to which you can attest. But this, sadly, involves a misspent logic. Why is the inability of your mother to recall your name any less horrific than her inability to paint any longer? Or to open a carton of milk? It is all a great rupture from the previous: the person you knew before is not the person confronting you *now*. And yet all of us create these portent lines of demarcation—once a person has crossed this threshold, say, well, things are truly bad. Well, *things are truly bad,* and there's no way around that.

And yet the need to create a personal graph of your loved one's dissolution is natural: if death is a problem for the living, since the dead one is clearly beyond all caring, the living-in-death aspect of Alzheimer's disease, which is how many people describe the illness, is clearly just a further embellishment of this truism. If one invests much of one's imaginative life in understanding others—if love is, as James Baldwin suggests, the difficult apprehension by one mind of the mysteries of another's life—then Alzheimer's clearly tests one's imaginative faculties. In some ways, the Alzheimer's loved one is the ideal subject to be modeled by one's graph; but just as one is about to make a truce with one's conception of the disease—just as the clay is about to set and hold the likeness, if you will—the disease irrefutably breaks the cast and leaves one dimwitted.

When I asked my mother my name, she quickly answered, "You *know* your name, why would you ask me that?" with that practiced New England refinement that both showed her mastery of the retort and her ability, at least here, to keep the conversation rolling. My mother didn't have the foggiest notion who I was or what her connection was to me, of that I am certain. But she had outwitted me—and she had kept her own distress to a minimum.

As time passed, and she became more and more remote, my mother talked less and less, and my visits were more and more occupied with combing her hair and doing things for her. Others could talk to their loved one without a response; I, because I am terribly self-conscious, could only with great difficulty commune with the ether, something of which I am not very proud. It is sad when at the most intimate of times, one still feels as if one's response is never adequate, as if one is still being judged. In truth, where there has once been her towering presence, there seemed to be increasingly my own pitiful falterings.

Still, one day, after my mother had been silent for a very long period, barely evidencing even the slightest flicker of acknowledgment, I brought her a teddy bear that I had purchased from LL Bean. It was a big red bear—with a lovely bib—and I knew that the color would arouse her, if nothing else. When I presented it to her, my mother took it, ruffled the ears, and smiled; for a second, she was returned to me. And then I, suddenly empowered, asked her, what she would name the bear, if she could call it anything.

In a shock of language, my mother replied, "I'd call the teddy bear Kenneth."

When she said this, I was near tears. Kenneth, of course, is my name and my father's name. For the last few months, my mother had shown no impulse to touch down with me; we had been together, but there had been no articulation on her part of our involvement; she had been as cut off from me as my brother's desire, many years ago, to become an astronaut.

"*This* planet is strange enough for me," I remember telling him, rather cruelly.

Now, I pushed onward. "Mom, why do you call the bear Kenneth?" I asked her. Her eyes softened and she answered, "It's a name I know well, and it's a name that comforts me. Your name is Kenneth." And then she grew quiet. She would never speak an intelligible word again.

My mother died in 1995 and my father was diagnosed with Alzheimer's in 1994. For one year, they both shared a room in a well-run nursing home in Falmouth, Massachusetts, although their relationship was, at least to my father, completely mystifying. Although they had been married for fifty-three years, and had raised three children, my father couldn't understand why he was living with this woman, with the lovely face and wild clothes. On one occasion he asked me, "Who is that woman; why is she always around?" And I had to stop myself from either laughing or crying. As I recall, I told him that she was his wife and that she and he had been together for many years, which I thought my father finally understood. But a few weeks later, in a rush of energy, my father informed me that he was going to marry someone, a friend of both my parents, and start a *new* family. And this was just the beginning of the story's complications.

My father had been a physician, and when he informed me that he was intending to marry Mary and begin a family, I was troubled, and not only because I had certain obligations to my mother, but because Mary was a good slice above 60 in age. Thus, her ability to have children was certainly a medical challenge, something that a younger Dr. McClane would have easily discerned. Interestingly, when confronted with the implication of having *two* wives, my father quickly told me that he had consulted with a lawyer, and the lawyer had told him that as long as he kept my mother with him, it would be fine to marry again. This reasoning, however opportunistic, was vintage my father. He would always try to please everyone;

and no one, in his world, was ever left bereft. As a doctor, with his office in Harlem, he had treated 75 percent of his patients gratis—they simply did not have the money to pay. And I well remember how his thankful patients would bring him pawn tickets, pies, and freshly caught fish—anything that might remotely be conceived as payment.

When I would walk around my neighborhood, people would often comment on how my father had saved a life, often thrusting the beneficiary, if it were a child, into my hands; one woman, wearing perfume that almost suffocated me, told me, through the vapors, "Your father is a *big* man; we're little people. He's God's face on the earth." Now, that was heady stuff!

Still, my father was a *good* doctor, although he would never speak about his work. I recall once when he came home mysteriously in the middle of the day, with blood covering his shirt, the stain resembling an errant Jackson Pollack painting. When I asked him what had happened, he told me it was "just work." I later learned that my father had literally held a man together with a towel. A number's runner had burst into my father's office, his guts tumbling out, and fell onto the receptionist, ruining her taffeta dress. The man had been brutally stabbed in the stomach because he had failed to honor a bet; and my father, seeing that the man was perilously close to dying and beyond anything that he in his office might do, grabbed a bath towel and tied it around the man's midsection, holding his innards in, until the ambulance came. The man survived, but two week's later, he was shot in the head—these things *happened* in my father's office, and he kept them secret, honoring a code of medical ethics, as ancient as it is draconian.

In the nursing home, my father had started to write Mary, his intended, salacious notes—which, of course, embarrassed her. These notes, interestingly, were in my father's usual handwriting—one could barely decipher every third word.

Yet Mary was right: my father was fantasizing about what he would like to do with her, even if it was, thank goodness, a fantasy of few connections. And so I was confronted with a very odd dilemma. In the first instance, I had never known my father to have a sexual fantasy life—which is as it should be. And in the second instance, my father never—and of this I am certain—ever cheated on my mother, or wanted to. So I was on very shaky ground. And then, too, Mary was a close friend and she felt decidedly uncomfortable. That both of us realized that my father was sick was of little help: we could only calibrate our response in the language of our own lives, which tended, hopefully, towards the rational. And Mary, of course, was in a much more difficult position than was I, since I had seen my father's progressive demise, and I did not have the same divided loyalty. Quintessentially, I was able to see my father as merely *otherbodied;* she, for her part, saw him as both her friend—which meant as he once was, in his verve and brilliance—and as the husband of someone whom she very much respected. She knew that *this* was not my father, but she couldn't figure out how to deal with the cipher before her.

My father's descent into the disease was horrible, in many ways, largely because he fought it so tenaciously. As he was losing his faculties, he, like my mother, learned to play to his strengths. As a doctor—and a very good one—he knew how to charm people. And, interestingly, his medical acumen was the last of his skills to leave him, with, just as tellingly, his ability to spin a good story. He might forget your name, but he would not forget how to diagnose a disease, or what to prescribe for a malady, which made his presence in the nursing home problematic. In short order, I made certain that my father had no access to prescription pads; Ms. Smith would not find an order for bursitis medicine, penned by Dr. Feelgood. And as luck would have it, just before my father became ill, he had coauthored an article on a rare form of hyperthyroidism, and it had received much notice in medical circles. When he talked to doctors—or anyone else who seemed interested—he would often mention the article, and they would be suitably impressed.

Indeed, early on, when I wanted a physician to diagnose my father's condition—I had seen signs of his mental impairment, which were worrisome to me—the doctor came to our house, began to talk to my father, and, lo and behold, after my father held forth about his article and the fact that he had recently retired from Columbia Presbyterian Hospital (where he had served on the medical school faculty for forty years), the diagnostician was clearly in his hands. When I asked the consultant for his recommendation about my father's acuity, he told me, "Your *father*, is there something wrong with your father?"

Here, of course, the physician was encountering a unique situation: first, my father knew how to keep the conversation anchored in a narrow channel that he had well learned to navigate, and my father was *truly* brilliant; even with a few synapses misfiring, he could astound and astonish; second, the doctor, understandably, was delighted to meet someone who knew more medicine than he did. Most doctors have not been exposed to the latest medical techniques; as my father used to tell me, "You're only as up-to-date as your last medical school class." Indisputably, my father has been at one of the premier medical schools in the world for the last umpteen years—he knew a great deal. And just as accurately, I do not believe that the consulting doctor could imagine that another doctor might be losing his faculties: it was simply too frightening a consequence to contemplate.

Getting my father to move to the nursing home was quite a feat, and I needed the help of my wife, my father's best friend, and a bold-faced lie. My father did not want to go to a nursing home: he loved his small house. For most members of his generation, your house—if you *owned* it—signified your achievement, even your personhood. Though a professional, my father held no stocks, bonds, or antiques: he simply had his home. To take it from him was, in truth, to remove something almost corporeal. At the time, my father was living on Martha's Vineyard Island, in a very efficient ranch home, with everything all on one floor, so he needn't struggle with stairs. But after he went missing for six hours on a very cold night, and was found by the police lying in a hedgerow a half block from his house, it was clear that the sixteen-hour-a-day, live-in staffing was no longer adequate to keep him safe. With an uncanny ability, my father would somehow find the one "soft spot" in our preparations: if we wanted to protect him, to keep him alive, he could no longer live at home.

On the day I planned to convince my father to enter the nursing home, I deployed a rigor of persuasive techniques worthy of Homer's Sirens, although at the time I simply felt despicable. Time permits you perspective, but perspective can't alleviate the horror of metaphorically pelting someone who seems inert, who, in his suffering, can only offer the most inglorious of supplications.

At first, my father's best friend, Bill Preston, asked him a few general questions: what is the day of the week, who is the president, and in which city did my father once work? Of course, my father did not have a clue, although he did try to offer a number of inventive explanations, which was both enormously poignant and sad. To see this formerly luminous man take small tentative stabs at reality, was heart-wrenching. At one point, my father began to talk about the New Deal with Rooseveltian fervor; and I almost believed that I was listening to a fireside chat when, like a whirlwind, my father migrated into a diatribe about John Kennedy's civil rights posture and then evolved into the small chapel where his father had once preached, which was a true remembrance, except that it suddenly found congress with an allusion to Tin Pan Alley. I tried to keep up, like a child chasing after a un-tethered kite, the trans-historicity was so spell-binding, and my father had just begun his peroration—details were colliding like sea-tossed stones: there was the FBI, Emmett Till, my wife, John Betti at BU, Adolph Jones, Duke Ellington, Boston Blackie, May Fane, the Federation of Protestant Agencies, the Kentucky Derby, Paul Robeson and World War II; there was Cornell University, Robert Scott, Elizabeth Taylor, Spinkie Alston (known as Charles), Dr. David Spain, Menemsha, clambakes, Block Island, Harvey Russell, Brigadoon (the house with the "big porch," he merrily added)—all congealing in a Whitmanic cumulus.

With a grim determinism that could only involve the warp and woof of love, Bill told my father how he had exhausted all our remedies, reminding him how he might have frozen to death had the police not been so zealous. Bill and my father had been inseparable for twenty years—they had shared countless fishing trips, suffered dreary near-football games (watching Columbia U. lose and lose and lose), and attended numberless civil rights benefits, where my father and Bill would often give brilliant exhortations, the money easily flowing, like curses at a juke joint. After his wife left him, Bill had lived in our home for a year, and he and my father were "spitting close," as my aunt would say. Bill, in fact, was the only man who could call my father an ass, and have my father learn from it. And my father did the same for Bill.

Bill's father had been the New York editor of the *International Herald Tribune,* but with seven children, it was often touch-and-go. Bill—who should have gone on to college, he read more deeply certainly than anyone I knew—worked so his siblings might have a better life. When the Second World War broke out, he enlisted. As a young boy, Bill had walked out of his parish after a "difficult confession" and never found use for God again. "Hard as a pool ball," he'd make it on his own, and the war, of course, just further cemented his detachment. "Ken," he told me, "no God could *permit* this carnage." If war would make everyone a believer, as it is often said, it did not do so for this lonely, wounded traveler.

As a tank sergeant, Bill had landed in North Africa, participated in D-day, and was waiting to go to Japan when the bomb dropped. When Bill had a few drinks, he would always return to the same tragic story. In Germany, his outfit had set up a perimeter around a fuel depot, near a grove of trees. Bill's tank was the lead one, and should there be any sound, it was his duty to ascertain what the commotion was. If it was suspicious, it was he who was to spray the area with his machine guns. One day, there was a slight ruffling in the trees, and Bill yelled, demanding to know who or what was present. There was no response. Quickly, he pummeled the field with bullets, leaving chunks of bark splayed on the ground like broken teeth. As he would always recount, he jumped out of his tank, grabbed his carbine, ran into the woods, and found a dead young girl, who had been scavenging for food. Bill had been in the war for three years, he'd killed hundreds of men, and liberated two concentration camps: he'd seen the worst human beings could do to one another. But that child's face was always with him, like a phantom limb. "She's only a child," he'd say, speaking unwittingly in the present tense; "Christ, she *is* only a child." When Bill would get into his story, my mother and father would hug him, and he would weep, hoping—inveterate atheist that he was—that the world might someday offer him a godless absolution. "I *killed* her," he'd say, over and over, the weight of it, as heavy as a vat of mercury.

"Ken," Bill said to my father, "you can't do this any longer. You've got to move. You can't do this yourself, to your son and his wife." When Bill finished talking, my father simply looked sullen, as if we had beaten him with sticks. Bill was his great friend, but friends could be wrong.

Then it was my wife Rochelle's turn. In her characteristically generous way, she suggested how much we loved my father, and how he would be able to have a better life, in a better situation, if he would move to the nursing home: he'd be able to travel with others, see recent plays, and possibly even go fishing, things he had always loved. Although my father was clearly listening to her, I couldn't tell if he was simply being the good, attentive father-in-law; his face was totally inscrutable.

After a time, Rochelle stopped talking, and my father smiled at her. I realized that he was trying to balance his great care for her, as he maintained his independence. Suddenly, I recalled how he would look as he straddled the small centerboard of our seventeen-foot sailboat when the boat would be coming about. At that magnificent moment when everything for a second stills and the sails luff, my father would hunker down, crumpling his big six-foot frame, waiting as the boom flew across, telling us in which direction we might proceed. Sailing, of course, is an art, and my father was very skillful at it. I never saw him frightened—the wind might be blowing, I often thought we might perish, but my father was simply engaged in the work.

Now, it was *my* turn to convince him, and I had one ploy, if only it might succeed. After recounting the dangers of my father's present situation, I reminded him of how he would wear his clothes all night long, so he wouldn't be found undressed when the senior citizen bus came. Since he couldn't tell time, my father would sport his jacket and trousers twenty-four hours a day, his clothes bedraggled, his shoes mismatched. My father was always prompt; he was never late; and he knew that the only way he could be ready for the bus—to look presentable—was to remain dressed all day. Seeing him struggling to measure up nearly stopped my heart: my father looked like a thin reed in a windstorm, his face so full of anticipation, his bearing, so tentative. After I had piled every stone of oratory on him, I suggested that he try the nursing home for one week. If he did not like it, we would bring him back home. And that's a promise.

In truth, I hoped that my father would not call me on the agreement—for once I placed him into the nursing home, he was not going to return. It was a terrible lie, and I hated to lie to him. But he accepted the bargain.

I well recall the journey to the nursing home, from one life to another. As we had so many times before, we took my father on the ferry from Vineyard Haven to Woods Hole, slicing between the picturesque East Chop and West Chop lighthouses, where we had often sailed in our small boat, and he talked to everyone he could on the ferry, telling them about his life and his family. My father was enormously proud of my wife and me, and as he recounted our tribulations, I felt great ambivalence. As always, people enjoyed him: he could tell a riveting story, and he wore his age well. Now, he was a wizened old man, and people rallied at the Norman Rockwellian ideal of the octogenarian, which possessed great power, no matter how hackneyed it might first appear. If it is sentimental, so are we; and thank goodness, we are.

After the ferry docked, we took the four-mile drive to Falmouth, where we had a wonderful dinner—of shrimp, his favorite—and went shopping for everything he might need: toiletries, new shoes, a bathrobe, stamps, and clothes that could easily be laundered. As always, my father was a raconteur. He spoke to all the salespeople, flattering them; he was in rare form, telling the salesgirls—always the *pretty* ones, as he would remark—something about his travels that day. His stories were always full-bodied, if not a bit freewheeling with fact. And then we entered the nursing home, and hoped that he would make a life there. My mother was already a patient, so he knew the place well. It was poignant to see him give her a small, winsome kiss on the lips.

At the end of that first day, just before we had to take the ferry back to the Vineyard, my father thanked us. "Ken, I had a wonderful first day," he said. And then, in the most generous act of a parent, he told me: "Ken, you did the *right* thing."

There it was, my parent of old—the one who would never place his wants before his child's smallest wish. I needed to hear that; I had felt, in truth, like Judas.

My father quickly made a life in the nursing home. Since he was a realist at heart, he knew that his faculties were deteriorating. He'd still charm the nursing staff, tell wonderful stories, and thrill any listeners with tales of Dr. Martin Luther King and other notables he knew. My father, here, was not fabricating: he and my mother had been directly involved in the civil rights movement on a national scale, and they had worked with the Southern Christian Leadership Conference, the NAACP, and the Committee on Africa. At our home, one might see Roy Wilkins, William Kunstler, and Ralph Bunche; Sydney Poitier came to my 10th birthday party, although he was most interested, I must admit, in the beautiful divorced parent of one of my friends.

It was not that my parents were extraordinary, or at least not in the way one might think: they were simply doing what they had to do as black professionals, who lived at a certain time, and who shouldered their weighty responsibilities. That my father also rented his office from Congressman Adam Clayton Powell gave him tremendous entrée into the world of the doers; that Congressman Powell, at every chance, also touted my father's medical acumen provided him with much-needed work, fellowship, and visibility. So, my father's stories were rich with luminaries, historical ephemera, and wonderment. His listeners, probably, thought that much of it was balderdash; but, in truth, there was a great deal of bedrock under his embellishments.

Indeed, it was these stories that were his last connection to the world to vanish. As my father became more and more sick, he grew thinner and thinner, and his stories grew less historically accurate; and yet, interestingly, they never failed to have a consistent beginning, middle, and end. However bizarre their content, they were always narratively complete—

that is, they were *good* narratives, and I'm speaking here as a teacher of writing.

In one of the most painful episodes I can recall, my father inquired about my brother, Paul, who had died twelve years earlier of alcoholism. Paul was a tough, truculent kid, who was enormously talented, but he did not love himself; or, more accurately, he loved others more than he did himself. In fact, he so identified with others that he almost chromosomally became them. Thus, if his friend was manic, Paul became manic. If his friend had a fight with his girlfriend, Paul's relationship with his sweetheart became perilous. In this odd transference, Paul's life seemed strangely to vanish, as if he existed only as a medium for others. "There was not enough of life left over to keep him around," a friend of his once said, and though I might quibble with the language, the sentiment was irrefutable.

When my father asked about Paul, I slowly explained that Paul had died a few years ago. Suddenly, my father began to wail, his once great shoulders slumped over. *Paul's dead, Paul's dead; I didn't know,* he murmured. Then he wailed again, his small ribs poking out like fish bones. *Paul's dead, Paul's dead,* as if this was the first time he had learned of his son's demise.

I realized that this revelation might occur daily—that in my father's besotted mind, he might each day relive his son's death. Each day my brother would die; each day my father would confront life's utmost devastation. It was horrible: Kafka could not have anticipated a more terrible scenario.

Yet, miraculously, the next day, my father had completely forgotten about Paul and our conversation. And he never returned to the subject again.

Alzheimer's disease wends its way rather predictably (although no one who lives through it can intuit this, for good reason), and I think of the disease metaphorically, as mirroring how one sees a landmass from an airplane. From a great height, everything is viewed as large sinews and great gentle curves: there are no rough edges to the shore, or ragged, ill-shaped promontories. With Alzheimer's, a person first loses her memory; then she loses control of her body; then she stops eating; and then, finally, she succumbs to an ultimate malady. One does not die of Alzheimer's: one dies of septicemia, pneumonia, or a heart attack. During this progression of diminishment, the person reacts in any number of ways—my mother, for example, when I brought her an easel and suggested that she might like to paint again, simply told me that she didn't need art anymore. When I asked her why, she told me that she "could see hundreds of trees and they were filled with dogs laughing." Now this vision, worthy of the best hallucinogens, aptly synthesized my mother's true enthusiasms: she loved dogs, and we had a number of them, to the great distress of my father. And just as poignantly, my mother always cherished gardening. Her mind, therefore, whatever else it was doing, was providing her with much satisfaction. If she was not in the world I understood, she was not unhappy. And this for me was a great dispensation.

Near the end of my father's life, his stories became far more impressionistic, and yet they would always meet the demands of a sturdy narrative. When I brought a number of family members to see my father, realizing that this was probably the last time that he would be at all present, the family ushered en masse into his room, talked with him for two hours, and made a wonderful fuss over him. His brother Warren was there—whom he hadn't seen in a year—and his niece, her son, my wife, and a few other people; it was a lively throng, and my father was holding court. At times, he would say things that were clearly appropriate: when he looked at his brother, he asked him, rather unfortunately, why he hadn't come to visit sooner. And I felt especially horribly for Warren, who, I knew, found confronting his brother in this state unbelievably painful. It had taken enormous courage for Warren to make the trip from New York City, and now he was being denounced. This, I think, in truth, was a brotherly confrontation, with a history that harkened back to Warren's birth placement as the youngest of four siblings, the baby of the family, who had always been beholden to my father, something that must have rankled Warren, too. In Alzheimer's, often a long ago rift finds a bizarre idealization: the disease is no respecter of persons or truth, but it does providently mine the fault lines, and it mines for lode. In a more conciliatory vein, my father asked his niece about her life, and he seemed to enjoy her passion for her new job. After a great deal of ballyhoo, my father simply dozed off, and we all departed.

The next day, pleased with last night's happenings, I asked my father about the family gathering, and he could not recall a thing. But then, almost as an afterthought, he began to describe a magical excursion, where he had visited an "enormous party," with hundreds of boats "dancing" in the harbor; there was a "great table," he joyfully added, replete with omnipresent shrimp for everyone. Shrimp, here, of course, was an expression of both his greatest delicacy and extravagance—when there was abundant shrimp at a salad bar, it was a true feast for this child of the depression. What most impressed him, he said, was that no one made him come in early. Clearly, something had pierced his isolation: it was not the true event; there was not one accurate detail. But my father had encountered something extraordinary, and it had brought him great pleasure.

I said at the outset of the memoir that I did not want my experience to be seen as representative of how Alzheimer's patients handle the disease or how families deal with their loved ones. Each family is different; the disease, I know, is horrific, and it can only bring unimaginable sorrow to a family, in ways that are specific, brutally intimate, and often disabling. Even the strongest family can flail apart under the enormous pressure of trying to conflate a wonderful past—or at least one where there was an assumed level of intimacy and identi-fication—with an increasingly distraught present. It is the height of horror to confront someone who has the shape, the smell, and the aspect of a person with whom you have shared your most intimate moments, and yet that person is merely a shell. It's like confronting a simulacrum of your father or brother or mother; and still—and this is both a blessing and a curse—he or she can suddenly blurt out a sound, or give you a slight nod, or make a shrill whistle-like noise, and the world is returned to a moment of clarity, of identification, where you once shared a glass of wine, or tried to fix the toaster, or simply collapsed into a hearty laugh. As A. R. Ammons asks in his poem, "What destruction am I blessed by?"

Near the end of my father's life, as he was sitting in the nursing home, he suddenly looked up at me, his head al-most jerking. "Ken," he said, "would you like to take a drive? We could drive down the West Side Highway and go to the Village." I knew what he was suggesting. My father worked six days a week, from 8:00 A.M. until 9:00 P.M., seeing patients. On our wonderful, rare outings, we would often travel to the Village, where we might get a sausage sandwich; or go to O'Henry's, where we might purchase a hamburger and he, a planters punch; or, most wonderfully, have paella at La Seville—a marvelous Spanish restaurant on Charles Street, where my father was treated as royalty. These were among the best moments of my childhood, when Paul and I, the boys, would be with our father. Interestingly, my mother would only rarely join us on these sojourns. I think she wanted us to have our father on our own terms—it was she, doing what she always did best, effectuating something, even if it demanded her orchestrated absence. It was, in Coltrane's terms, "a love supreme," since I know how much she missed us, even for those few moments.

I thought for a second about my father's proposition. I could, of course, remind him that there was no automobile, that we were in a Massachusetts nursing home, and that he was near the end of his days—I could tell him that. But I was *driving* with my father, the car was slowly snaking from our Harlem brownstone, down Riverside Drive, and we'd soon cross over 72nd Street to get to the West Side Highway, we'd brush along the Hudson River until 23rd Street, and then we'd turn and go down 7th Avenue, which would be full of people hawking wares—and possibly a street concert would provide us with congas, or violins, or a tender drift of Brahms; there might be a small art show near St. Mark's Place, and he'd comment on how much better my mother painted; but I could also sense, for the first time, my father's growing impatience with the transgressive jaywalkers—he was tight in the shoulders, his breath labored—and so I suggested, with great tenderness, "Dad. Let's swing by Central Park. It's lovely this time of year."